LEGAL PSYCHOLOGY

LEGAL PSYCHOLOGY

Eyewitness Testimony
Jury Behavior

By

L. CRAIG PARKER, JR., Ph.D.

Psychologist and Associate Professor
Division of Criminal Justice
University of New Haven
West Haven, Connecticut

CHARLES C THOMAS • PUBLISHER
Springfield • Illinois • U.S.A.

Published and Distributed Throughout the World by
CHARLES C THOMAS • PUBLISHER
BANNERSTONE HOUSE
301-327 East Lawrence Avenue, Springfield, Illinois, U.S.A.

© *1980, by* CHARLES C THOMAS • PUBLISHER
ISBN 0-398-04054-0
Library of Congress Catalog Card Number: 79-27365

With THOMAS BOOKS *careful attention is given to all details of
manufacturing and design. It is the Publisher's desire to present
books that are satisfactory as to their physical qualities and artistic
possibilities and appropriate for their particular use.* THOMAS
BOOKS *will be true to those laws of quality that assure a good
name and good will.*

Printed in the United States of America
N-1

Library of Congress Cataloging in Publication Data

Parker, L. Craig.
    Legal psychology.

    Bibliography: p.
    Includes indexes.
    1. Psychology, Forensic.   2. Witnesses—United States.
3. Jury—United States.   I. Title.
KF8922.P37   347.73'66   79-27365
ISBN 0-398-04054-0

*To my daughter, Jennifer,
the youngest student of
eyewitness testimony I know.*

ACKNOWLEDGMENTS

A NUMBER of individuals read the manuscript and offered helpful comments. Stephen Dreyfuss, a New York Assistant District Attorney, reacted not only to the legal aspects but went through the material much like an editor. My friend and colleague, Lynn Monahan, also offered comments on the structure and organization of the material, in addition to responding from her frame of reference as a psychologist. I'm also indebted to attorneys Lloyd Goodrow and John Quinn who read the entire manuscript and offered their views.

Virginia and Lawrence Parker read the manuscript and I appreciate their assistance.

Finally, I am grateful to have had the opportunity for research and study at Columbia University School of Law. During the 1977-78 academic year, when I was appointed as a Visiting Scholar, I was able to immerse myself in the research required for the preparation of this text. Officials at Columbia University's School of Law were also helpful in arranging my association with Judge Harold Rothwax at Manhattan Supreme Court. The opportunity to observe proceedings at Manhattan Supreme Court and to interact with various functionaries of the Criminal Justice system was invaluable.

L.C.P.

CONTENTS

LEGAL PSYCHOLOGY

Chapter I

THE PSYCHOLOGY-LAW INTERFACE

OVERVIEW

IN RECENT YEARS there has been a revival of interest in the psychology-law area, drawing its sustenance from the ranks of psychologists. The work of Tapp (1976-1977), and Levine and Tapp (1973) has helped to chart not only the early history of the relationship but current developments as well. Tapp (1976) has used the term *interstitial* to describe the relationship of these two fields. She has observed that while they have coexisted side by side, there has been limited interaction between them. Even today, while increasing numbers of psychologists have become interested in law and criminal justice, there is little movement in the other direction. Few lawyers are actively seeking out psychologists or consulting scholarly psychological literature.

As of this writing, only two psychology-law programs exist in America. The first program was initiated at the University of Nebraska several years ago and it has been served by both the law school and the psychology department, while the second program has sprung up at the University of Maryland in recent months. The whole question of the relationship of the behavioral sciences to law becomes further clouded if psychology's cousin, psychiatry, is brought into the picture. Similar to psychology, psychiatry has struggled to develop a working relationship with law. Some later comments by Judge David Bazelon of the United States Court of Appeals for the District of Columbia Court will help to illustrate the status of psychiatry as it relates to mental health issues and the court.

When representatives of the two fields engage in direct contact with one another, these contacts usher in feelings of hostility and indifference, as well as openness and receptivity. The history of the relationship is extremely uneven. Few law schools have any behavioral or social science faculty among their ranks. One prominent psychologist, after completing a year as a Visiting Professor at a prestigious West Coast law school, remarked, "They regard us as journalists."

An examination of a recent law school text on *Evidence* (Maguire, Weinstein, Chadbourn and Mansfield, 1973) indicates that while very limited coverage is given to psychological issues, sources and references are provided for the ambitious student who is prepared to investigate the phenomena on his own. The text described in detail one series of experiments conducted by lawyer Marshall (1966) as he sought to demonstrate some of the weaknesses in eyewitness reports.

One final anecdote is revealing. During a conversation that the author initiated with a Federal judge, who also happens to be a faculty member at a prestigious law school, the question was asked, "What do you think about the use of psychologists in jury selection?" "Not much," barked the judge, as he stormed off, refusing to discuss the matter further.

In contrast, and atypical I might add as far as legal education is concerned, Yale Law School offers a variety of subjects in which law and social science theory are interwoven. An example, for instance, is the course entitled *Scientific and Experimental Evidence*.

Buckhout (1977) opened an address to the New England Psychological Association's annual conference by noting that from the perspective of lawyers and judges, psychologists are "walking in the province of the judge and jury as finders of fact." On the other side of the coin, one can understand the disappointment and anger of the judiciary as they try to decipher the hieroglyphics of the psychiatrists' and psychologists' reports they must examine in order to render judgments in various cases. In general, lawyers remain highly skeptical of the value of experimental psychological laboratory evidence. One nationally known criminal law professor refuses to pay any attention to social-psychological experiments, although the findings bear directly on the course that he teaches.

Psychiatrists and Psychologists As Expert Witnesses

My recent experience as a Visiting Scholar at Columbia University Law School allowed me to spend some time with a number of Manhattan judges involved with criminal felony cases. I came to understand quickly their lack of respect for psychiatrists and psychologists. In addition to the criticism that these professionals obscure their main points with excessive jargon, it seems that many who appeared on a regular basis prostituted their talents to whoever was paying the bill. Judges viewed them as local "hired guns" who could be counted on to do what was expected of them by their sponsors. Undoubtedly the most eminent member of the judiciary to concern himself with the activities of psychologists and psychiatrists in the courtroom has been Judge David Bazelon of the United States Court of Appeals for the District of Columbia Circuit.

In writing on the subject of behavioral experts (Bazelon, 1974), he laments the failure of psychiatrists to provide clear and concise diagnostic assessments. He describes judges' patient attempts to educate psychiatrists concerning what the legal system requires of behavioral/medical analysis. In addition, he describes (Bazelon, 1974) the general difficulty in getting many "expert witnesses" to translate their scientific analysis into understandable English when he says, "I have seen our familiar judicial procedures attempt to bring the most arcane sciences and technology under public surveillance. Psychiatry, I suppose, is the ultimate wizardry. My experience has shown that in no case is it more difficult to elicit productive and reliable expert testimony than in cases that call on the knowledge and practice of psychiatry" (p. 18). One of the key problems as he notes in the *Scientific American* article (Bazelon, 1974), is that they try to limit their testimony to *conclusory* statements rather than focusing on the facts of the case that they should be knowledgeable about. By attempting to pre-empt the function of the judge and/or the jury as the final arbiter of a conflict, they demonstrate a lack of appreciation for the adversary system of justice.

In the American system, the "expert" is allowed to make a judgment or conclusion. The mechanic can state that the car had defective brakes before it left the repair shop; he is fair game, however, for extensive cross-examination concerning the facts he relied upon to reach that conclusion. Mental health professionals are far more eager to pin on the label of "schizophrenic" than they are to describe the facts that buttress this conclusion.

Part of this problem, of course, is tied fundamentally to the limited knowledge of human behavior that is available. I am referring to the limited hard evidence that has accumulated, notwithstanding the great number of studies and articles that have been published on the subject. For years, mental health experts have vastly oversold their product in the marketplace. Consumer conscious groups, such as those spearheaded by Ralph Nader, have moved to demand greater accountability. They have pressed psychotherapists to spell out their services and to provide timetables for the length of treatment for their patients. The mystique of psychiatry has been fueled by the exorbitant fees ($50.00 an hour) that many charge and the M.D. or Ph.D. credential tacked on the wall.

In the case of *Durham* in 1954, Bazelon (1974) believed his opinion had provided a vehicle for psychiatrists to structure their testimony differently. Many psychiatrists appeared to welcome it. The so-called "Durham rule" provided a framework for a new test of criminal responsibility. The Durham case held that an accused individual is not criminally responsible if it is shown that his unlawful act was the product of a mental disease or defect. It was designed to allow behavioral experts (particularly psychiatrists) to bring into the courtroom their *knowledge* of the case but to return to the jury its historical role of applying "our inherited ideas of moral responsibility" (Bazelon, 1974). This effort failed to encourage behavioral experts to offer their thesis to the court in a useful manner.

In 1972, the *Brawner* decision set aside the *Durham* rule. In a unanimous opinion, the United States Court of Appeals for the District of Columbia Circuit drew on the insanity test that had been proposed by the American Law Institute. This view was that "a person is not responsible for criminal conduct if at the time of such conduct as a result of mental disease or defect he lacks substantial capacity either to appreciate the wrongfulness of his conduct or to conform his conduct to the requirements of the law."

This standard was an attempt, once again, to structure expert witness testimony in such a fashion that it would no longer be controlling over the question of moral responsibility, the jury's function. Bazelon (1974) nonetheless remained pessimistic about the psychiatrists' willingness to forego offering conclusory testimony. His own separate opinion in *Brawner* suggested that the jury be instructed that a defendant is not responsible "if at the time of his unlawful conduct his mental or emotional processes or behavior controls were impaired to such an extent that he cannot justly be held responsible." This statement, of course, has obvious implications for the psychologist, along with other mental health professionals such as the social worker.

The opinion was designed to encourage a broad range of information concerning the accused as reflected in the language which was not distinctly medical. Bazelon's separate opinion in this case was not related to his earlier experience with the American Psychiatric Association, in which that organization attempted to restrict other professionals from participating in courtroom proceedings as expert witnesses.

The *Jenkins* case, in 1962, prevented psychiatrists from squeezing psychologists out of the picture. While the American Psychiatric Association attempted to argue that psychologists were not competent to render an expert opinion on the issue of mental disease, the court held that qualified psychologists could give expert testimony and that the critical inquiry concerned the actual experience and qualifications of the psychologist, which in turn would affect the probative value of his opinion. One of the frequently occurring phenomena associated with expert testimony in this area, the battle of the experts in which psychiatrists for each side take differing stands, is deeply flawed because of some of the above-mentioned problems.

Donald Lunde (1975) in his book entitled *Murder and Madness* discusses some of his views on the role of the psychiatrist in the courtroom. He illustrates why there is such a credibility problem when it comes to expert mental health witnesses:

In practice court-appointed psychiatrists are often not impartial; in fact, some judges will appoint specific psychiatrists recommended by the prosecution and known to have almost perfect records of finding every defendant sane. Often such court-appointed psychiatrists have the same employer as the prosecutor (the state) for they are frequently on the staff of a state mental hospital or work for some government agency. Their opinions are filed with the court before the trial begins. If they find the defendant to be sane, they will subsequently be called as witnesses for the prosecution at the trial. Less often, a court-appointed psychiatrist may find a defendant insane, in which case he may be called as a witness for the defense. In many cases, attorneys for the prosecution and defense will consult privately with as many potential psychiatric witnesses as necessary (when they can afford it) until they find one or two whose opinion they deem useful to their side (p. 120).

With this type of approach characteristic of courtroom conflict, the lack of respect for mental health expertise is understandable. While the legal community appears distressed with the performance of mental health experts (principally psychiatrists) does this explain its rigidity concerning the acceptance of bona fide scientific psychological evidence as it bears on problems such as eyewitness testimony, jury processes, and lie detection? It appears that jurists have been far too skeptical and cautious in responding to empirically based psychological evidence. Needless to say, the cause of justice would be advanced if the courts were able to discriminate between those areas in which behavioral science has little to offer and those in which it has something significant to offer.

One need only read of the early attempts on the part of Hutchins and Slesinger (1928, 1929) to influence the law in the areas of "evidence" to sense what a short distance we have come. Recently, Robert Hutchins expressed his disappointment concerning the minimal impact of his work on the law of evidence over the past thirty-five years (Tapp, 1976).

Psychology, Law and Society

In addition to offering a contribution to the "action settings," including courts, mental health facilities, and correctional institutions, Kolasa (1972) views the psychologist as potentially able to assist in the general dialogue concerning the role of law in society. He comments: "Today the most fundamental task for the behavioral scientist with respect to the functioning under legal structures may well be that of determining the factors underlying the social and legal order. Then one can proceed to the utilization of the information as the basis for decision making in specific and individual situations. In the determinaton of relationships, the behavioral scientist aids in the making of legal policy" (p. 499). Tapp (1977) has also been concerned about the legal structure and its relationship to "socialization." She has developed her views to a much greater extent than Kolasa (1972) and offers quite a different perspective. Her evolving theory examines the way in which the individual comes to understand and incorporate legal concepts in the context of socialization.

Much of Pospisil's (1971) work on the anthropology of law concerns the way in which law becomes interwoven in the developing individual's consciousness. Typical of an anthropological approach, Pospisil states that his approach to studying law is not culture bound. In his work, Pospisil focuses on the process in which psychological factors play a role in the "internalization" of law. In reviewing the learning theory of Dollard and Miller, he notes that this offers one explanation for the way in which the individual confronts the law. By virtue of one response being reinforced as opposed to another, the individual's behavior changes in the direction of the rewarded activity. Piaget's theory is also offered as a possible explanation for the way in which a child developmentally adapts to the social structure of his parents and peers.

This anthropologist, however, seems to place his major emphasis on a paradigm of social influence that is offered by Kellman (1966). Three qualitatively different processes (compliance, identification and internalization) are presented as offering the framework and are defined generally as follows:

(1) *Compliance* is overt acceptance induced by expectation of rewards and an attempt to avoid possible punishment, not by any conviction in the desirability of the enforced rule.

(2) *Identification* is an acceptance of a rule not because of its intrinsic value and appeal but because of a person's desire to

maintain membership in a group or relationship with the agent. The agent is attractive and this appeal provides the power for the relationship.

(3) *A special type of identification (identification with the aggressor)* happens, although an individual may initially hate the agent as an oppressor, and even torturer. Identification with this person does take place, and positive feelings toward the tyrant do develop. This results because the individual tries to cope with his frustration and anxiety by mastering the object of the frustration.

(4) *Internalization* results in the acceptance by an individual of a rule or behavior because he finds its contents intrinsically rewarding. The power that serves this mechanism is the individual's conviction of the desirability of the prescribed conduct.

Hogan (1970, 1972) has offered an approach which integrates concepts of law and morality. While drawing on the work of Piaget (1965) and Kohlberg (1963) to explore developmental phenomena, Hogan departed from their structured sequential view of development to include the effects of socialization. He was interested in the way underlying personality structure was predictive of moral choices. After empirically establishing two approaches, "the ethics of personal conscience" and "the ethics of social responsibility," he proceeded to correlate these philosophical approaches to personality data gathered on a variety of subjects. Certain clusters emerged. Supporters of the "ethics of personal conscience" tended to be progressive, rebellious, and unconventional. They may also be undependable and capricious according to Hogan. Those whose views are characterized by "the ethics of social responsibility" appear guided by rational and legal considerations and are therefore often thoughtful, considerate, and honest. However, their personalities are also characterized by traits of conventionalism and overconforming behavior. They present a strong need for structure and order. They are oriented toward positions in which rules of conduct are viewed as constructive.

In a separate research study on the relationship of personality to moral-legal reasoning, Hogan and Dickstein (1972) sought to expand further their preliminary findings. In this study, the authors employed a projective test in which subjects were required to complete short statements on matters involving social and moral issues. Scores from this device were correlated with responses from the Survey of Ethical Attitudes. The authors found support for their hypotheses that the ethics of personal conscience were related to a tendency to blame and distrust institutions while the ethics of social responsibility were related to a suspicious attitude toward others. In other words, those *legally* minded individuals appeared to be responding to their distrust of their fellow man by establishing rules to control and curb behavior. In contrast, those individuals whose moral reasoning is characterized by intuition and a "case by case" analysis presented a more benevolent attitude toward man. The latter group were more inclined to perceive the roots of injustice as being located in *institutions,* while the former group (who rely on law and social regulation) identified the *individual* as the culprit.

An equally exciting, although very different, approach to evaluating perceptions of justice lies in the work of Thibaut, Walker, LaTour, and Houlden (1974). These investigators, using Rawls' theory of justice as a springboard, designed an experiment to tap subjects' underlying philosophies of justice. They presented individuals with various choices of models of conflict resolution, ranging from *inquisitorial* to *adversarial* systems. Typically, the *pure inquisitorial* model is characterized by control of the decision-making process in the hands of a single individual. It included "an activist decision maker directly developing the facts in interaction with involved persons and then reaching and announcing a decision" (p. 1273).

Midway on the continuum is the model of the *double investigator.* Here the decision maker is less active because he is assisted by two investigators. Each is required to investigate the contentions of the disputing parties and is required to report the facts to the decision maker for judgment. An example would be the courtmartial of the U. S. Military. The variant on the other end of the spectrum is the *bargaining* model. This approach, which is fundamentally adversarial, is primarily under the control of the disputants. It is different from the adversarial system as exemplified by the American system of civil procedure in that disputants meet without the intervention of a third party. The most common example of this approach is the "plea bargaining" in criminal cases. The researchers designed an experiment in which some of the participants were aware of the side they were on in the legal dispute, while others were ignorant of the role they were to play. The thrust of the study was directed at the question of which model of justice was preferable to the participants. The results demonstrated that all subjects identified the amount of decision-making control to decrease steadily from the *inquisitorial* to the *adversarial* procedure. In general, subjects expressed greatest preference for the *adversarial* procedure. This was also related to judgments of the *adversarial* procedure as being the fairest mechanism. Subjects who were not participating in a given role for a particular side chose a perspective that led them to prefer, as a judgment of fairness, systems that "they believed to favor the disadvantaged while tending to preserve equal access to channels of information and to mechanisms of control" (p. 1288).

On an applied social action level, the Justice Department is experimenting with "Neighborhood Justice Centers" (McGillis, 1977). This project was prompted by the extensive court backlogs and by the theory that the courts are both an expensive as well as a severe means of conflict resolution. While the Justice Centers focused on minor disputes and employed lowkeyed techniques for dealing with conflicts, "binding arbitration" was sometimes used when mediation efforts failed.

A different intervention into legal issues on the part of psychologists is reflected in the use and interpretation of social science surveys. These include attitude surveys and "opinion polls." In a later chapter, the author will address himself to the way in which survey data are employed by psychologists assisting defense counsel in the selection of jurors. Recently, Vidmar and Ellsworth (1974) probed survey data on the death penalty. They noted that the public's attitude on this highly controversial issue was not unimportant to members of the U. S. Supreme Court when the *Furman* decision was handed down. *Furman v. Georgia* held that the death penalty, as then administered, violated the eighth amendment's prohibition of "cruel and unusual" punishment. The Stanford University scholars took the position that merely noting general levels of support for or against capital punishment, via nationwide polls and surveys, did not provide the kind of information needed to judge what the public really wanted concerning the death penalty. After sorting through the many surveys and polls that have been launched on this subject over the past ten years, and by examining, also, some studies that correlated attitudes toward the death penalty with personality data, they (Vidmar and Ellsworth, 1974) reached some tentative conclusions:

> First, despite the increasing approval for the death penalty reflected in opinion polls during the last decade, there is evidence that many people supporting the general idea of capital punishment want its administration to depend on the circumstances of the case, the character of the defendant, or both, rather than on the kind of non-discretionary death penalty permissible under *Furman*.
>
> Second, there is evidence that at least some of the support for capital punishment may stem from motives that are inconsistent with contemporary legislative and judicial goals. Some people may support the death penalty primarily for motives of retribution; supporters of capital punishment, moreover, are more likely than opponents to endorse attitude statements supporting prejudice and discrimination, violence as a means for achieving social goals, and restrictions on civil liberties (p. 1267).

Developments in the field of jury research have been deferred for later chapters and will be discussed at great length. Psychologists are currently active on a number of other frontiers. Monahan (1976, 1977) has written extensively on the subject of mental health and law. A number of scholars have been interested in the way in which children have become involved in legal proceedings (Woody, 1977) and in their perceptions of law (Keasey and Sales, 1977).

In reviewing the contributions of psychology in the area of testimony, Judge Jack B. Weinstein of the U. S. District Court in Brooklyn (1957) took an extremely dim view not only of the historical contributions of the behavioral sciences, but of future prospects as well. In his opening statement, he concluded "superficially, the study of testimony appears to offer a rich field for sociologists and psychologists. In fact, the probability is low of any change in our trial institutions because of new insights from these disciplines" (p. 6).

Writing in the same special issue of *The Journal of Social Issues,* Fishman (1957) reviewed some "needs" in the psychology of testimony. He singled out witness credibility as an issue that deserved much greater attention. He reasoned that due to the interest in witness accuracy, i.e. eyewitness testimony, a number of additional issues had been ignored. Claiming the battle between psychologists and lawyers concerning the use of psychological evidence to be a "pseudo" issue, he suggested that while the legal community was reluctant to credit the findings of psychologists, they nevertheless had frequently been adopted as court reforms had evolved.

Psychology and Criminal Justice Education

Unquestionably, one of the most active fields for psychologists has been the criminal justice educational arena. With the large-scale funding provided by the U. S. Department of Justice under the Law Enforcement Assistance Administration (L.E.A.A.), psychologists along with criminologists, forensic scientists, lawyers and others have found employment on the faculties of criminal justice degree programs. These programs serve police officers, corrections personnel, probation officers and other functionaries of the criminal justice system. In addition to the teaching function, faculty have initiated research and engaged in consulting with police departments and correctional agencies.

As with any large-scale Federal support, many institutions developed programs merely to attract funding. Consequently, large numbers of these programs have offered dismal academic instruction as a result. Two factors appear to have been critically related to this situation. First, the L.E.A.A. exercised no quality control over the programs, and second, congressmen were quick to support a local institution's program if it was attacked, regardless of its academic caliber.

The problems of utilizing the most up-to-date scientific findings in the search for justice has many parallels in other fields. People on the frontiers of knowledge frequently observe an extended time lag before the "establishment" is prepared to accept their contributions and innovations. One of the major purposes of this book is to help close further the gap between experimental evidence and its application in the courtroom. It is hoped that lawyers, judges, police, probation officers, psychologists and others will find it of value. In addition to focusing on the eyewitness problem, the book will address the controversial issue of social scientists and jury selection, along with the issues involved in jury decision-making.

HISTORICAL DEVELOPMENTS

Much of the early history of legal psychology was dominated by the efforts of psychologists to interest lawyers in their experimental work, which they felt had implications for the courtroom. While today much of the psychological work that relates to law involves jury selection, jury decision making, child custody, socialization, rehabilitation of offenders, police behavior, mental health issues, patients' rights, and lie detection issues, earlier interest was focused on the law of evidence and eyewitness testimony.

Freud (1906) attempted to assist the legal community in making determinations of the truthfulness of witnesses. Drawing on his understanding of unconscious processes, he suggested that judges and lawyers be alert to "slips of the tongue" and other unusual responses of criminals. He compared criminals with psychoneurotics in pointing to hidden material when he noted: "In the case of the criminal it is a secret which he knows and hides from you, but in the case of the hysteric it is a secret hidden from him, a secret he himself does not know" (p. 18). Elsewhere in his paper he warns lawyers and judges to be aware of (1) "unusual content in the reaction which requires explanation," (2) "increase of reaction-time, for stimulus- words which have touched the complex area reacted to after considerable delay," and (3) "faulty reproduction" (p. 17).

Munsterberg (1908) is considered to be one of the pioneers of legal psychology in the United States. While perhaps best known for his work on the psychology of the courtroom (Moskowitz, 1977), Munsterberg was also known for his work in philosophy and film criticism. Munsterberg enjoyed the controversy that surrounded his entrance onto the legal stage and his class work, *On*

The Witness Stand, (Munsterberg, 1908) offered some sharp criticism of attorneys for their reluctance to draw on psychological findings:

> The lawyer and the judge and the juryman are sure that they do not need the experimental psychologist. They do not wish to see that in this field preeminently applied experimental psychology has made strong strides, led by Binet, Stern, Lipmann, Jung, Wertheiner, Gross, Sommer, Aschaffenburg, and other scholars. They go on thinking that their legal instinct and their common sense supplies them with all that is needed and somewhat more; and if the time is ever to come when even the jurist is to show some concession to the spirit of modern psychology, public opinion will have to exert some pressure (p. 10-11).

Munsterberg's views have become known beyond the confines of academe as he frequently wrote for the lay audience. Concerning perceptual processes, Munsterberg cleverly devised experiments with his students at Harvard that helped illuminate the problems inherent in eyewitness accounts. In one instance he requested several hundred students attending a lecture to write down answers as accurately as they could to a number of questions posed on exhibits presented (Munsterberg, 1908). He randomly selected one hundred answers for analysis. Initially, he showed them a large sheet of white cardboard on which fifty little black squares were posted in irregular order. He exposed it for five seconds and then inquired as to the number of spots on the sheet. Responses varied between twenty-five and two hundred. A second question involved judging the perception of time. He asked students to give the number of seconds that passed between "two loud clicks." While the actual time span was ten seconds, responses varied between half a second and sixty seconds, with a good number of students offering forty-five seconds as the correct time. In another experiment he asked students to identify a sound. Only two of the hundred answers he examined correctly identified the sound as a tuning fork. Other experiments demonstrated the weaknesses in memory.

Today, many authorities on eyewitness testimony point to the reconstructive aspects of eyewitness accounts in which individuals unwittingly add to the original perception. Munsterberg accurately determined this from his observations and experiments at the turn of the century. He states, (Munsterberg, 1908), "Yes, we fill the blanks of our perceptions constantly with bits of reproduced memory material and take those reproductions for immediate impressions." While much of his writing was popular rather than scientific, his accounts of well-intentioned individuals' inaccurate descriptions of various events laid the groundwork for more serious study of sensory phenomena as they relate to legal proceedings. As Moskowitz (1977) notes in his article on the place of Munsterberg's work in the history of psychology:

> Eventually, the psychiatrist and psychologist would appear regularly as "expert witnesses" in criminal trials. The polygraph and psychological assessment would become standard techniques in criminal investigation. And psychological training would become a major part of programs in the administration of justice and a popular elective in law schools and prelaw programs (p. 833).

It is interesting, in light of the present day literature on eyewitness testimony, to note that Whipple (1909) was wrestling with some of the same key issues that divide psychologists and jurists today. He commented, "The experimental method possesses the obvious advantages, standardization of conditions, control of the determining factors, possibility of repetition and of quantitative and statistical evaluation of the results. But the method has been criticized, particularly by jurists, on the ground of oversimplification, general artificiality and consequent nonapplicability to the problems of real life—criticism which is, I think, entirely intelligible, however incorrect" (p. 155). A number of key issues such as the form of questioning of the witness (narrative vs. interrogatory), the choice of questions, age and intelligence of subjects, estimates of the duration of events, and the effect of repeating a report were studied by Whipple.

Whipple's survey of research on these phenomena (although the research designs and statistical analyses were unsophisticated by today's standards) were fundamentally consistent with present day findings (Whipple, 1909, 1912). For instance, dramatic differences emerged in the accuracy of reports offered by direct eyewitnesses as compared to individuals who relayed reports from others (the fundamental problem of rumor). The overestimation of time by most individuals who observe an event for a brief period was noted along with the strong suggestibility of children. His later paper (Whipple, 1912) focused on studies designed to train witnesses to improve their performances in reporting events accurately. The value of these studies, however, as vehicles for understanding eyewitness testimony at criminal proceedings appears to be seriously limited, if for no other reason than that the subjects ranged between ages eleven and thirteen.

Gross (1911) ventured into the wilderness of the psychology-law area with his early volume on *Criminal Psychology*. This work, perhaps mistitled, focused on a great variety of human behavior in the courtroom. Not only was Gross concerned about the behavior of "criminals" but of witnesses, jurors and judges. Originally appearing in German, it drew primarily on Gross' own observations of human behavior, which while interesting were of limited value. He occasionally drew on references from the behavioral scientists of the day. It is interesting that the committee of the American Institute of Criminal Law and Criminology that chose to sponsor this as part of a series of translations of important works was made up primarily of law professors and lacked a psychologist among its membership. Furthermore, and more importantly, the work of Gross, a German criminal law professor, was their selection in the *psychological* area. The eminent Dean Wigmore was on this committee, and his jousting with psychologist Munsterberg was a matter of record by that time (Wigmore, 1909).

William Marston (1924) engaged in research on the subject of testimony and his studies anticipated the main findings of scholars at a much later date (Buckhout, 1974; Goldstein, 1977; Wall, 1965). Like others, including Munsterberg (1908) and Trankell (1972), he arranged for a lecture audience of eighteen lawyers to witness an "incident." The incident, presented as a spontaneous happening, involved a young man entering the class while Marston was lecturing. The youth then proceeded to hand some papers to Marston, and after a brief conversation, drew a pen knife. Immediately after the incident, the audience's perception of the event was obtained. Later, a second similar experiment involving twelve lawyers was conducted, but this time the participants were told to expect the episode.

Generally, Marston found that *free narration* was less complete than either *direct* or *cross-examination*. In addition, *direct examination* was determined to be both more complete and more accurate than *cross-examination*. He observed that the entire group of witnesses under "expected" conditions, as contrasted with the whole group under "unexpected" conditions demonstrated a slight gain in completeness during all types of report (ranging from 4.5% to 8.8%), but they showed a slight loss in accuracy in all types of testimony (averaging 7.9%). Finally, the reduced caution of the group under "expected" conditions appears to have reduced their accuracy. Perhaps the most important finding was that, after breaking down the episode into a number of details, witnesses generally provided very incomplete testimony. Percentages for completeness were: 23:2 (free narration), 31.2 (direct examination) and 28.7 (cross-examination).

Finally, Marston was interested in evaluating "which finder of fact can produce more accurate results for purposes of comparison with witnesses' testimony, judge or jury?" In this instance, he found the judge to be more accurate. When written versus oral testimony were compared, the experimental jurors' finding was superior for written testimony. However, it should be noted that Dean Wigmore, perhaps the most highly esteemed scholar of evidence of that time, had been selected to act as the judge in this experiment.

Also in 1924, a study by Cady (1924) appeared in the *American Journal of Psychology*. She reported on an experiment in which a confederate of the researcher appeared briefly before classes of students to announce various requirements for positions that were open in the government and foreign service fields. One group was asked to provide a *narrative* account of all the events that took place during the man's presentation, while a second group was asked a series of highly *specific questions*. A greater number of errors were found among responses to *specific questions,* and the range of the *narrative* reports covered many more details (88) than the *specific question* reports (50). The researchers, in summarizing the results, observed that the largest number of errors were associated with very particular information presented along with "facts which we habitually treat in some stand-ardized manner."

Other scholars such as Whitely and McGeoch (1927), Burtt (1931), McCarty (1929), and Stern (1939) engaged in legal-psychological analysis. Whitely and McGeoch (1927) investigated the effect of one form of report on another. Drawing on students at Washington University, the researchers arranged for three experimental conditions: "simple narrative," "simple interrogatory," and "narrative plus interrogatory." They found that for the "simple narrative" condition, retention fell quite rapidly for the first ninety days, and then more slowly for the period from ninety to 120 days. When the interrogatory condition (specific questions and answers) was presented immediately after the narrative condition, the subsequent narrative recall was improved for 30, 60, 90, and 120 days.

In the late 1920s, a series of articles appeared on the psychology of evidence (Hutchins and Slesinger, 1928, 1929). Sensitive to the early criticism of Munsterberg because he was "too confident and overshot his mark," these co-authors presented a less generalized and less aggressive attack on the law. Lawyer Hutchins and psychologist Slesinger seemed more intent on encouraging the legal community to adopt a more flexible response to emergent psychological research. Slesinger was perhaps the first psychologist ever appointed to a law faculty when he was added to the staff of the Yale Law School by Robert Hutchins, who was Acting Dean at that time (*New York Times,* 1977).

One unique contribution offered by the Hutchins-Slesinger team (Hutchins and Slesinger, 1929) was their psychological analysis of a number of assumptions related to the law of evidence. For instance, concerning "spontaneous exclamations," they stated, "Though the courts are clearly headed in the right direction in holding that statements made under sudden shock will not often be intentional fabrications, they do not observe that emotion at the same time so impairs objective accuracy that the report of an excited individual is not likely to be worthy of much credit" (p. 17). While praising the courts for taking into account the obvious loss of memory over a period of time, they were quick to point out that the law erroneously assumed that forgetting took place at a constant rate. They were interested in the court's treatment of "habit" and they observed inconsistent policy in this area. They noted:

> Although habit is usually not allowed to evidence a given act, it is regarded as a great guarantee of accuracy in one instance. One may not show that a witness habitually tells the truth in order to show that he is telling the truth on the stand. But one may get in evidence his account books or business entries regularly made on the ground that the accuracy of these is guaranteed by his habit of making accurate records (p. 19).

Concerning one of the most difficult and yet important areas, the authors pointed to the fact that in some instances courts did not allow the previous history of criminal acts to be "allowed in" as proof of the commission of a similar act. Many jurisdictions provide sweeping protections to juveniles when it comes to preventing the prosecution from citing their previous illegal acts committed at an earlier age. Hutchins and Slesinger (1929) viewed this policy as excluding the most relevant and persuasive psychological evidence.

Finally, they raised the question of whether the adversarial system of justice was really the most effective one for determining the truth, particularly as it was reflected in the aggressive confrontation of witnesses. The debate on this most central of all issues continues to this day, with psychologists attempting to study the issue through empirical scientific methods (Thibaut and Walker, 1975). While not openly castigating lawyers for their reluctance to accept psychological findings, they chided the eminent Dean Wigmore for stating that "when the psychologists have anything to offer, the law will be ready for them" (Hutchins and Slesinger, 1929, p. 21).

McCarty (1929) came along afterwards with his work on *Psychology For The Lawyer*. Like Gross' work, it claimed to be a work on psychology, and similar to Gross, McCarty was a lawyer with no formal training in psychology. The comparison stops, however, at this point. Relying much less on anecdotal material and his own judgment, McCarty thoroughly reviewed the psychological literature available to him in the late twenties. Although there was limited empirical evidence to support his contentions,

McCarty was able to articulate the way in which bias and prejudice found their way into legal proceedings. His analysis of eyewitness problems raised issues that are now familiar to the student
of that subject. Unlike some of his contemporaries, he presented
a balanced approach neither overstating nor undervaluing psychological data.

Burtt's (1931) work on *Legal Psychology* represented the first
major work on psychology-law by a psychologist since Munsterberg's work in 1908. Burtt made far fewer claims for psychology
than his colleague had originally offered. He thoroughly reviewed
the theory and research available at the time, and his comprehensive treatment of the subject appeared to be highly regarded in
legal as well as psychological circles. It should be noted that
Munsterberg (1908) had been taken to task by Wigmore (1911),
who accused the Harvard psychologist of acting irresponsibly in
stating that lawyers were "obdurate" and unwilling to accept the
precise knowledge that had been made available to them. In a
cleverly-worded satirical piece appearing in the *Illinois Law
Review* (1911) , Wigmore successfully destroyed Munsterberg's
main contentions that lawyers had rejected widely known psychological information, and that the exactness of psychological knowledge claimed by Munsterberg was factual.

Burtt (1931) , however, did not overreach in describing what
psychology had to offer, and his approach to lawyers was more
conciliatory. In his preface discussing his purpose for writing, he
noted:

> Perhaps the initial motive was the need for a textbook for the
> aforementioned university course *(Legal Psychology)*. Subsequently,
> however, the conviction has developed that there was a much larger
> field for such a work among the members of the legal profession. As
> scientific principles are established, the law gradually takes cognizance
> of them. It is felt that the science of psychology has developed a very
> considerable number of principles bearing on legal problems that
> are worth presenting (p. 211).

Burtt (1931) was one of the first scholars to discuss the way in
which emotions could disrupt eyewitness testimony. His theory
was that emotion interfered with accurate perception during the

period it was experienced, as well as immediately after the event. Quoting the German, Jaffa (1913), he reported that, experimentally, in a highly emotional incident, there was a 17 percent increase in errors. Burtt also offered several cases to illustrate his point. He concluded that it would be much better if emotions were absent.

A recent article by Buckhout (1974) pointed to the problem of dim lighting and the impact it had on a case involving eyewitness testimony. Burtt identified this problem in 1931 by citing how experimental evidence demonstrated that severe perceptual distortions were commonplace under poor lighting conditions. His work touched on many problems of interest to students of legal psychology. They included problems of the emotionally disturbed, confessions, drugs, crime prevention, memory, perception, hypnotism, and jury decision-making processes.

An article entitled "The Perception and Memory of Wisnesses" appeared in 1933. The author, a member of the North Carolina Bar, was sympathetic to the scientific findings offered by psychologists (Gardner, 1933). Noting that juries quite generally regarded the assertiveness and positiveness of the witness as a barometer of his credibility, Gardner was quick to point out that the confidence of the witness, no matter how genuinely expressed, was far from any guarantee of the truthfulness of testimony. He reviewed a great many findings concerning perception and memory processes. The key points culled by Gardner from his review of literature on memory included:

> We tend to remember what we observe or recall frequently. The more recent the experience, the better the memory of it. The more vivid, striking or impressive the scene, the clearer and more retentive the memory of it. We remember best what we like, next what we dislike, and poorest of all those things to which we are indifferent (p. 392-396).

It was obvious to this lawyer that some of the experimental work on memory, including that of Ebbinghaus on nonsense syllables, had limited value to the practicing attorney. He found Dallenbach's work on memory of a picture or scene more useful for lawyers. He concluded his analysis of memory by commenting that faulty memory could be attacked most effectively along three distinct lines:

(1) The original perception of the event or detail may have been defective.

(2) The details may not have been fixated, may have been forgotten, or imagination may have altered, added to, or changed them.

(3) The original perception may have become interwoven with or altered by suggestion from outside sources (p. 408).

The German psychologist, William Stern (1939), gave a lecture to the Open Forum of the Psychologists' League on December 29, 1937, in which he recounted his experiments with students and offered opinions concerning the psychology of testimony. Stern was adamant about the ability of psychologists to contribute to the legal process, and his implied criticism of the legal profession for not being more receptive to what psychologists had to offer was reminiscent of Munsterberg's views. His experiments supported the already widely held notion that in addition to memory loss over time, witnesses tend to unwittingly reconstruct the original situation. His work did result in amendments in German law on procedures involving the admission of evidence.

As the reader may have inferred from much of this first chapter, a definition of legal psychology presents a certain awkwardness. In a fundamental sense, it appears to be that area of psychology which concerns itself with legal issues and problems. It defines an emerging branch of psychology. While this chapter has focused on the historical development of the psychology-law relationship, it is interesting to note the limited use of the term "legal psychology." Burtt (1931) entitled his comprehensive text *Legal Psychology,* but until the publication of Toch's (1961) work on *Legal and Criminal Psychology,* no other major work employed that rubric. Hutchins and Slesinger (1929) entitled one of their articles "Legal Psychology," but otherwise the use of the phrase in the literature is limited.

Toch's (1961) definition was as follows: "Legal psychology as a science studies the process whereby justice is arrived at, examines the people who take part in this process, and looks into their purposes, motives, thoughts and feelings. As a profession, legal psychology aims at reducing to a minimum those psychological factors which detract from the objectivity of the legal process. The final aim is to make justice as fair and constructive as possible" (p. 3).

Toch's definition is cumbersome as well as inaccurate, particularly for what it excludes, but it typifies the problem of presenting a succinct and precise definition. However, Toch (1961) and his collaborators prepared the only major text in this general area over the last forty years, excluding a spate of texts since 1976. In offering what was admittedly a loosely connected series of chapters, editor Toch, in collaboration with a number of social scientists and lawyers, covered a wide range of topics. Their book read much like an introductory survey to the subject of legal psychology. The materials, while not offering new empirical research findings, provided a variety of theories and commentary on such diverse subjects as, "Trial Tactics in Criminal Cases," "The Psychology of Juries," "The Psychology of Judges," "Criminal Responsibility and Psychiatry," "The Gauging of Criminal Predispositions," "Psychologists and Juvenile Delinquency" and "The Sex Offender and His Treatment."

Of the various chapters presented, Winick's (1961) work on the "psychology of juries" was particularly interesting and represented one of the first efforts of a psychologist to examine issues in this field. It may be recalled that Marston (1924) had engaged in some jury simulations, determining that females were better than male jurors and that written evidence was superior to oral evidence. Winick's account reviewed work at Yale in which researchers (employing jury simulations) found that judges' instructions to disregard certain testimony had little effect, and that an indictment, notwithstanding a judge's efforts to limit its prejudicial value, tended to make the defendant suspect. Finally, as was generally known, juries tended to disregard the rules of law.

Summary

In this first chapter, the author has provided an overview of the psychology-law interface. In addition to discussing current developments in the field, a historical perspective has been offered. A recurrent theme of the early history of legal psychology was the attempt on the part of psychologists to make an impact on the law. While psychologists today have focused on a much broader array of psycholegal concerns, the early history was marked by a pronounced interest in the psychology of testimony.

REFERENCES

Bazelon, D.L. Psychiatrists and the Adversary Process. *Scientific American,* 1974, 230, 18-23.

Bettèlheim, B. Individual and Mass Behavior in Extreme Situations. *Journal of Abnormal and Social Psychology,* 1943, 38, 417-452.

Buckhout, R. Eyewitness Testimony. *Scientific American,* 1974, 231, 23-31.

Buckhout, R. *Eyewitness Percpetion, Identification and Recognition.* Paper presented at New England Psychological Association Conference, Worcester, Massachusetts, November 5, 1977.

Burtt, H.E. *Legal Psychology.* New York: Prentice Hall, 1931.

Cady, H.M. On the Psychology of Testimony. *American Journal of Psychology,* 1924, 35, 110-112.

Fishman, J.A. Some Current Research Needs in the Psychology of Testimony. *Journal of Social Issues,* 1957, 13, 60-67.

Freud, S. Psycho-Analysis and the Ascertaining of Truth in Courts of Law. In *Collected Papers,* (J. Rivière translation), 1953, 2, 13-24.

Gardner, D.S. The Perception and Memory of Witness. *Cornell Law Quarterly,* 1933, 18, 391-409.

Goldstein, A.V. The Fallibility of the Eyewitness: Psychological Evidence. In B.D. Sales (Ed.), *Psychology In the Legal Process.* New York: Spectrum Publications, Inc., 1977.

Gross, H. *Criminal Psychology.* Boston: Little Brown & Company, 1911.

Hogan, R. A Dimension of Moral Judgment. *Journal of Consulting and Clinical Psychology,* 1970, 35, 205-212.

Hogan, R., and Dickstein, E. Moral Judgment and Perceptions of Injustice, *Journal of Personality and Social Psychology,* 1972, 23, 409-413.

Hovsland, C.I., Janis, I.L., and Kelley, H. *Communication and Persuasion: Psychological Studies of Opinion Change.* New Haven: Yale University Press, 1968.

Hutchins, R.M. and Slesinger, D. Some Observations on the Law of Evidence—Memory. *Harvard Law Review,* 1928, 41, 860-873.

Hutchins, R.M. and Slesinger, D. Legal Psychology. *Psychology Review,* 1929, 36, 13-26.

Jaffa, S. Ein psychologusche Experiment in Kriminal Seminar der Universitat Berlin. *Bertrage zor Psychologie der Aussage,* 1913, 1, 79-100.

Keasey, C.B. and Sales, B.D. Children's Concept of Internationality and the Criminal Law. In B.D. Sales (Ed.) *Psychology in the Legal Process.*

New York: Spectrum Publications, Inc., 1977.

Kellman, H.C. Compliance, Identification and Internalization: Three Processes of Attitude Change. In H. Proshansky and B. Seidenberg (Eds.) *Basic Studies in Social Psychology.* New York: Holt, Rinehart & Winston, 1966, 140-148.

Kohlberg, L. The Development of Children's Orientation Toward a Moral Order, *Vita Humana,* 1963, 11-33.

Kolasa, B. Psychology and Law. *American Psychologist,* 1972, 27, 499-503.

Levine, F.J. and Tapp, J.L. The Psychology of Criminal Identification: The Gap from Wade to Kirby. *University of Pennsylvania Law Review,* 1973, 121, 1079-1131.

Lunde, D.T. *Murder and Madness,* Stanford, California: The Portable Stanford, Stanford Alumni Association, 1975.

Maguire, J.M., Weinstein, J.B., Chadbourn, J.H. and Mansfield, J.H., *Cases and Materials on Evidence.* Mineola, New York: The Foundation Press, 1973.

Marshall, J. *Law and Psychology in Conflict.* Indianapolis: Bobbs Merrill, 1966.

Marston, W. Studies in Testimony. *Journal of Criminal Law and Criminology,* 1924, 15, 5.

McCarty, D.G. *Psychology For The Lawyer.* New York: Prentice Hall, 1929.

McGillis, D. *Neighborhood Justice Centers As Potential Models for Dispute Resolution.* Paper presented at New England Psychological Association Conference, Worcester, Massachusetts, November 5, 1977.

Monahan, J. *Community Mental Health and the Criminal Justice System.* New York: Pergamon Press, 1976.

Monahan, J. Social Accountability: Preface to an Integrated Theory of Criminal and Mental Health Sanctions. In B.D. Sales (Ed.) *Perspectives in Law and Psychology: The Criminal Justice System.* New York: Plenum Press, 1977.

Moskowitz, M.J. and Munsterberg, Hugo A study in the History of Applied Psychology, *American Psychologist,* 1977, 32, 824-836.

Munsterberg, H. *On the Witness Stand: Essays on Psychology and Crime.* New York: Clark Boardman, 1908.

N. Y. Times, Donald Slesinger, A Psychologist and Ex-Law School Dean Is Dead. October 14, 1977.

Piaget, J. *The Moral Judgment of the Child.* New York: Free Press of Glencoe, 1965.

Pospisil, L. *Anthropology of Law: A Comparative Theory.* New York: Harper & Row, 1971.

Roven, B. Social Influence and Power. In I.D. Stiner and M. Fishbein (Eds.) *Current Studies in Social Psychology.* New York: Holt, Rinehart

& Winston, 1965, 371-382.

Sales, B.D. *Perspective in Law and Psychology: The Criminal Justice System.* Volume I., New York: Plenum, 1977.

Stern, W. The Psychology of Testimony. *Journal of Abnormal and Social Psychology,* 1939, 34, 3-20.

Tapp, J.L. Psychology and the Law: An Overture. In M.R. Rosenzweig and L.W. Porter (Eds.), *Annual Review of Psychology,* Volume 27, Palo Alto, California: Annual Reviews, 1976.

Tapp, J.L. Psychology and Law. In B.D. Sales (Ed.) *Psychology In The Legal Process.* New York: Spectrum Publications, Inc., 1977.

Thibaut, J. and Walker, L. *Procedural Justice: A Psychological Analysis.* Hildsdale, New Jersey, Lawrence Erlbaum Associates, 1975.

Thibaut, J., Walker, L., Latour, S., and Houlden, P. Procedural Justice As Fairness. *Stanford Law Review,* 1974, 26, 1271-1289.

Toch, M. *Legal and Criminal Psychology.* New York: Holt, Rinehart & Winston, 1961.

Trankell, A. *Reliability of Evidence.* Stockholm, Sweden: Beckmans, 1972.

Vidmar, N., and Ellsworth, P. Public Opinion and the Death Penalty. *Stanford Law Review,* 1974, 26, 1245-1270.

Wall, P.M. *Eyewitness Identification in Criminal Cases.* Springfield, Illinois: Charles C Thomas, Publisher, 1965.

Weinstein, J.B. The Law's Attempt To Obtain Useful Testimony. *Journal of Social Issues,* 1957, 13, 6-11.

Whipple, G.M. The Observer As Reporter: A Survey of the "Psychology of Testimony." *The Psychological Bulletin,* 1909, 6, 153-170.

Whipple, G.M. Psychology of Testimony and Report. *Psychological Bulletin,* 1912, 9, 264-269.

Whitely, P.L. and McGeoch, J.A. The Effect of One Form of Report Upon Another. *American Journal of Psychology,* 1927, 38, 280-284.

Wigmore, J.H. The Psychology of Testimony. *Illinois Law Review,* 1909, 3, 399-434.

Winick, C. The Psychology of Juries. In H. Toch (Ed.) *Legal and Criminal Psychology.* New York: Holt, Rinehart & Winston, 1961.

Woody, R.H. Psychologists in Child Custody. In B.D. Sales (Ed.) *Psychology in the Legal Process.* New York: Spectrum Publications, Inc., 1977.

Chapter II

EYEWITNESS TESTIMONY: PSYCHOLOGICAL PERSPECTIVES

INTRODUCTION

ALTHOUGH the matter of eyewitness testimony has occupied the attention of legal psychologists as much as any issue, it continues to be controversial. From the psychological side, Munsterberg's (1908) early work set the stage for subsequent opinion and experimentation, but legal scholars, of course, have a much longer history of venturing into these troubled waters. Wall (1965) offered the most comprehensive statement on the subject. He was a lawyer by training but his analysis also incorporated the psychological issues as well.

While the recent decade saw the United States Supreme Court attempt to untangle the issues in *United States v. Wade* (1967), *Gilbert v. California* (1967), *Stovall v. Denno* (1967), *Kirby v. Illinois* (1971), and *Moore v. Illinois* (1977), the Court's views have vacillated over this period. While the Court in *Wade* (1967) directly confronted the serious weaknesses in many eyewitness accounts, the majority opinion in *Kirby* (1971) undercut the Court's earlier sense of the problem. *Moore* (1977) appears to merely clarify some of the earlier pronouncements.

As noted earlier, Wall (1965) embraced some of the key psychological dimensions, as well as legal ones, in his classic work, *Eye-Witness Identification in Criminal Cases*. The importance of the topic is framed when Wall (1965) offers: "The influence of improper suggestion upon identifying witnesses probably accounts for more miscarriages of justice than any other single factor—perhaps it is responsible for more such errors than all other factors

29

combined" (p. 26).

There is a gap between the general acknowledgement of the seriousness of the problem of eyewitness accounts, as offered by members of the judiciary, and actual courtroom practice. That is to say, judges and particularly juries seem insensitive to the actual flimsiness of the testimony of witnesses as reflected in the weight they place on evidence of this type. It has been stated frequently that far too great a premium has been placed on eyewitness testimony at the expense of other evidence.

Miller and Boster (1975) sought to compare the weight given two different eyewitness accounts of a murder in contrast with that given to a confession, and that given a key piece of circumstantial evidence (a weapon which belonged to a certain party who was working in the same office on the night of the murder). Their experimental procedure included providing a brief description of the background of the incident along with a statement concerning the motivation of the suspect. Not surprisingly, subjects who were asked to assume that they were jurors rated the confession highest in terms of a guilty findings (4.55 on a scale of 6.00), followed by the eyewitness account in which both parties were known to the witness (4:30), the circumstantial evidence (4.15), and finally, the unfamiliar witness condition (3.89). As the mean scores indicate, all types of evidence were given significant weight.

One scholar (Goldstein, 1977) recently commented that courts should adopt a rule in which eyewitness reports, uncorroborated by additional evidence, should not be admitted into evidence. It is questionable if this rule is the right medicine to cope with the power of the myth of eyewitness infallibility. Obviously, a more searching inquiry of the nature of an eyewitness report(s) in a specific case, given the present scientific evidence available, might require that in some instances eyewitness testimony be buttressed by additional information, but this might not always be necessary. This inability on the part of the judge and jury to exercise discretion, under Goldstein's rule, might present more problems than it solves.

Speculation on the fundamental matter of why so much weight is afforded a person's eyewitness account of an occurrence leads to the conclusion that a self-serving psychology operates. People hate to believe that they can be wrong. Conventional wisdom suggests that "seeing is believing" and that any individual who claims to have observed a particular event with his own eyes and who provides an intelligible account should be trusted. Many of us, of course, notwithstanding our attempts at honesty, remain unaware of how perceptual distortions and prejudices intrude themselves into our narrations of events. Add to the mixture the losses and constructive effects of memory and the likelihood of obtaining a "videotaped replay" on the part of a human being is vastly reduced. In addition to the convincing quality of witnesses (who many times are certain that they are giving totally accurate accounts), some are pillars of society and their prestige in the community is persuasive. Or perhaps it is the encounter in the courtroom in which the witness dramatically points to the defendant and exclaims, "That's the man! That's him! I could never forget his face!" (Buckhout, 1974, p. 23). Regardless, both sides—prosecution and defense—confidently predict success when they have an eyewitness.

History has demonstrated (Borchard, 1932; Rolph, 1957) that there are instances in which as many as seventeen witnesses were ultimately proven to be wrong in their identifications of suspects. Rolph (1957) has chronicled the classic misidentifications of a number of persons, including Adolf Beck, Oscar Slater, and a trio of alleged offenders—Emery, Thompson and Powers. In the introduction to the case of Oscar Slater, Rolph arouses the reader's interest by asking him to envision what it would be like if one imagined oneself accused of a crime committed three months earlier. A person had raised such an issue with Rolph as a "cure for insomnia." The account is presented as follows:

> "Imagine," he said, "that you are unjustly accused of having murdered someone three months ago exactly. Circumstantially, the case against you is absolutely complete, and yet you are innocent. Do you admit that such a thing is possible? I knew that it was, and said so. "Then instead of counting sheep," he said, "try to work out what you were doing on the day of the murder, and what witnesses you can call to prove it. If you keep on reminding yourself that you are faced with a murder charge, it's wonderful the way it keeps your mind on the job. What sends you to sleep is the concentration of thought on a hopelessly elusive purpose." What I did

find was that by establishing salient points of recollection—a journey, a party, a theatre, an illness—you could get much nearer to the actual date than you might suppose; but I never once established a single fact about the vital date itself. It was the implications of all this that kept me awake. (p. 93)

Throughout history, there are numerous examples of well-intentioned, even courageous, acts by individuals who have refused to go along with the party line, attempted to correct mistakes, or reform entrenched bureaucracies. Their efforts have not infrequently cost them their jobs, or a worse fate has resulted. A Lieutenant John Trench, in the case of Oscar Slater, proved to be such a person (Borchard, 1932). His involvement was both instrumental in Slater's conviction as well as in his ultimate release.

Briefly, Slater was accused of murdering an eighty-three-year-old woman. Police were given general descriptions offered by a servant and a man who lived in an apartment just below the victim. Four or five days after circulars were sent out describing the wanted man, the police picked up a clue that led them to Oscar Slater. The suspect was known to have earned his money from the sale of jewels and gambling. He had attempted to sell a diamond broach fitting the general description of one missing from the victim's home. Slater was arrested in New York and extradited to Great Britain for trial. The two original witnesses, in addition to a third witness (a fifteen-year-old girl who had come forth later and claimed the accused had brushed against her on his way out of the apartment) were asked if they could identify Slater in New York at a "show-up." A show-up is an event in which witnesses are asked to identify a suspect with no other candidates present. It is obviously a very suggestive process and one which has been criticized extensively by both lawyers and behavioral scientists over the years.

Two of the witnesses offered an immediate identification of Oscar Slater. Later, after Slater had been returned to Great Britain, the prosecution presented twelve additional witnesses who claimed to have seen Slater loitering in the vicinity of the victim's apartment. All, with varying degrees of certainty, identified Slater. While unable to give a clear alibi, Slater was able to describe his activities and associations in detail on the critical day.

Nonetheless, he was convicted and remained in prison for eighteen years, until enough gaps and weaknesses in the original case, along with subsequent evidence, were brought to light to cause his release. It seems that among other things, the lineup that was presented for the group of twelve witnesses contained a large majority of police officers who did not resemble the suspect. All the witnesses had been exposed previously to a photograph of Slater, thus further biasing their evaluations. The police officer at the lineup, Lieutenant Trench, readily admitted that Slater might have been picked out easily because he was the only "foreigner" with a dark complexion. This matched the general description which had been circulated. Trench's own doubts about his role in the government's case led to his uncovering additional bits of information which ultimately led to Slater's release. The prosecutorial forces, however, were unhappy with Trench's assistance in the cause of justice and he was dismissed from the police force. In a more positive vein, as a result of extensive publicity of the case, a Court of Criminal Appeal was established in Scotland to review such cases (Bochard, 1932; Rolph, 1957).

While the problems of personal identification in the Slater case arose in 1912, a reminder that the issue continues to plague the criminal justice system is offered in the case of Barry Moskowitz circa 1978 (Raab, 1978). It is doubtful that even if all the proposed remedies offered to insure fairness in the handling of eyewitness identification cases were adopted, the large majority of all such cases could be fully resolved. The fact that conscientious and honest people will continue to differ in their reporting of their observations of a crime is one of those immutable phenomena that will exist as long as man. Attempts to harness irrational and biased means of procuring convictions in these cases will continue, and additional reforms appear to be within the reach of technology and the courts, but some cases of mistaken identification are inherently unresolvable. The frustration and sense of uncertainty which characterized the case of Barry Moskowitz is an example (Raab, 1978).

Barry Moskowitz, a twenty-one-year-old Brooklyn College senior, was convicted in one of New York City's largest bank robberies ($279,000) primarily on the basis of conflicting eyewitness testimony. The bank heist occurred on June 3, 1976, and none of the loot has been recovered as of this writing, two years later. Someone with what appeared to be "inside" knowledge of the Chemical Bank's operations approached the bank's branch manager just before he was to open for business at 9 A.M. at the branch office in the Sheepshead Bay section of Brooklyn. The unmasked robber, armed with a pistol and hand grenade, confronted the manager as he started to enter the door of the bank. Later testimony revealed that the robber knew the family of the manager, a Mr. Gleason, and threatened to harm his family if he did not cooperate. The thief seemed to be knowledgeable concerning the bank's procedures, including which bank employees were familiar with the combinations to the bank vault. The holdup man also avoided bank cameras; and his behavior indicated that he was aware of the fact that two bags, containing a large amount of money in small denominations, were ready for pickup on that day.

To many, young Moskowitz seemed an unlikely suspect. In addition to attending Brooklyn College, he was an auxiliary police officer with ten citations. He had applied for a police officer position with the Port Authority of New York. Varied descriptions were given of the robber. Manager Gleason and others agreed that he had blond or dark blond hair and a blond mustache. Descriptions of his age and height were discrepant with the facts. Significantly, none of the witnesses' descriptions mentioned the robber's complexion—Moskowitz had severe acne.

Using a police artist's sketch of the suspect (a composite of descriptions offered by the witnesses), bank personnel compared videotaped pictures of bank customers. Three employees thought Moskowitz resembled the holdup man. After locating the individual in question as Moskowitz, he was surveilled for two months.

The suspect claimed that he had slept until noon on the morning of the robbery. However, that afternoon he flew to Florida on what he claimed was a week of vacation, planned much earlier. At the time of arrest, the suspect was viewed in a lineup with six other mustachioed men. Two identified Barry Moskowitz, while two others identified an F.B.I. agent. The fifth person said the perpetrator was not in the lineup.

At the trial, the manager, who had had the longest exposure to the offender, clearly identified Moskowitz. A second employee was less certain. She had initially identified an F.B.I. agent in the lineup, and her original description of the perpetrator did not match Moskowitz. A clerk, offered as a third prosecution witness, admitted that her description had differed from Moskowitz'. Finally, another employee, who had observed the robber's face for an estimated three seconds, stated that Moskowitz was not the person in question.

In pulling together the elements of the case, the prosecutor emphasized that Moskowitz never returned to the Chemical Bank for business (although he had previously been a regular customer), and that he had purchased a one-way ticket to Florida.

On the defense side, it was brought out that Moskowitz used a bank in Manhattan after the robbery because he had been working in that borough on the James Buckley campaign staff. Furthermore, the defense lawyer argued that many people at Buckley's headquarters had known of Barry's intended vacation in Florida well in advance of the robbery. The defendant claimed that on two occasions he was approached by prosecutorial staff offering to drop or reduce charges in exchange for his implicating organized crime figures believed to be behind the heist. Recently, in passing sentence, a judge, noting Moskowitz' excellent background, placed him on probation.

Concerning the way in which juries magnify the importance of eyewitness accounts, Borchard (1932) wrote:

> Perhaps the major source of these errors is an identification of the accused by the victim of a crime of violence. This mistake was practically alone responsible for twenty-nine of these convictions [sixty-five cases of innocent parties convicted were studied by the author]. Juries seem disposed more readily to credit the veracity and reliability of the victim of an outrage than any amount of contradictory evidence by or on behalf of the accused, whether by way of alibi, character witnesses, or other testimony. These cases illustrate the fact that the emotional balance of the victim or eyewitness is so disturbed by his extraordinary experience that his powers of perception become distorted and his identification is frequently most untrustworthy. (p. xiii).

A more modern day student of the subject, Robert Buckhout

Legal Psychology

(1974), has commented, "It is discouraging to note that the essential findings on the unreliability of eyewitness testimony were made by Hugo Munsterberg nearly eighty years ago, and yet the practice of basing a case on eyewitness testimony and trying to persuade a jury that such testimony is superior to circumstantial evidence continues to this day. The fact is that both types of evidence involve areas of doubt" (p. 31).

A problem not reported historically with any frequency, however, is the one posed by the fearful or indifferent witness. The infamous Kitty Genovese case of 1964, in which more than thirty-eight neighbors observed the slaying of a young woman from their apartment windows, is cited as the classic case of individuals who "did not want to get involved." A flurry of social psychological experiments on the subject of "bystander apathy" followed, in which social scientists tried to shed light on the factors that contributed to this type of situation.

Recently, the *New York Times* (McG. Thomas, 1977) reported on a crime in Brooklyn in which as many as fifty friends of the victim observed his murder. After repeated and intensive efforts by an Italian police officer to encourage witnesses to come forth, some members of the Italian community agreed to testify. The problem of reluctant witnesses is a prevalent one according to an attorney in the Manhattan District Attorney's office (Personal Communication, Assistant District Attorney Stephen Dreyfuss). He states that it poses one of the major stumbling blocks to successful prosecution of cases.

The remainder of this chapter is devoted to reviewing pertinent literature on memory and perceptual processes, discussing pertinent social-psychological experiments, and establishing the general psychological foundations for eyewitness accounts. While many of the distortions of eyewitness accounts occur as a function of perceptual or recollection processes, a third important area has to do with the communication of the experience—what Marshall (1963) refers to as *articulation*.

PERCEPTION THEORY AND RESEARCH

Notwithstanding lawyers' reluctance to embrace psychological literature on eyewitness testimony, knowledge concerning memory has continued to expand (Hilgard, Atkinson and Atkinson, 1975; Gerard, 1953; Murdock, 1973; Wertheimer, 1973; Morgan, 1974; Burner, 1958, 1973). As Levine and Tapp (1973) have noted, "We all know from our experience—and psychologists from their professional training and practice—that people quite often do not see or hear things which are presented clearly to their senses, see or hear things which are not there, do not remember things which have happened to them, and remember things which did not happen" (p. 1088).

One place to start this discussion is by asking, "Why is perception fallible?" To answer this question, let's begin by examining what perceptual processes are. Morgan (1974) relates perception to the experiencing of sensations. He states:

> People perceive objects, not just collections of stimuli, and object perception is determined in part by innate organizing tendencies. These include the tendency to perceive a figure on a ground, the tendency to group objects together, and the tendency to create closure—to fill in missing elements. Stability in our perceptual world is maintained largely through perceptual constancies in shape, size, and brightness. Depth perception relies on both monocular and binocular cues. The principal monocular cues are linear perspective, clearness, interposition, shadows, texture, and movement. The main binocular cue is retinal disparity of the images seen by the two eyes. Motion perception can consist of either real or apparent motion (p. 204).

A less physiological definition is offered by Bruner (1958, 1973), who focused on the social psychological factors which impinged on the individual and color his perceptions. A person's needs, values and early childrearing experiences are viewed as critical in affecting his view of the world. Personality dynamics, the social status of the individual, and the selectivity of perception are topics of interest to the "new look" school of perception (Bruner, 1973).

Wertheimer (1973) has also stressed the active role of the perceiver in the formation of a percept and commented on the creative aspect. He noted:

> But of all the stimuli reaching our sense organs, only a small fraction are acted upon, and this acting upon is very much a function of the perceiver's characteristics—attention, past experience, memory and

social and cultural factors. The active role of the perceiver is also a
very creative one; we do not simply accept or reject a percept that is
entirely determined by stimulus characteristics. Instead, we create
percepts from the information we have, and this information is
partly sensory, partly personal, and partly social. We may even
create a percept with no sensory input at all, as in the case of hal-
lucinations. (p. 601)

Experiments involving group pressure conducted by Asche
(1955) and others have helped to document the manner in which
individuals' opinions—related to their perceptions of events—can
be altered.

The Nature of Perception

Before reviewing studies that bear on the social psychological
features of perception, a brief review of current theory concerning
the structural or organic basis of perception would appear to be
appropriate. Introductory material on this subject appears to fit,
generally, the definition offered by Morgan (1974). Basic princi-
ples of perception tend to stress the processes by which individuals
organize their perceptual fields and include the mechanisms that
are believed to play a role in figure-ground perception, grouping,
shape and size constancy, color constancy, movement perception,
depth perception and visual coding devices.

A basic characteristic of people's perception is the relationship
of *figure* and *ground*. Research on individuals who have had cor-
rective surgery to remedy lifelong blindness demonstrates that
even for these individuals, the figure-ground relationship is present, although other features are missing (Hilgard, Atkinson and
Atkinson, 1975).

Another organizing tendency involves the organism's *grouping*
of stimuli. One item is identified as part of another, or in close
proximity to it. Grouping may occur in response to similarity,
symmetry or continuity. The Gestalt notion of the sum of the
parts being different from the whole applies here. Gestalt psychologists have historically been interested in *closure,* and the desire
for closure results in a person's organizing his world into patterns.
These patterns are thought to emerge in response to the individual's expectations and social experience, as much as from the

physiological structure of the eye and brain. Throughout any analysis of perception, one finds an interaction between the eye, the brain, and the environment. Wertheimer (1973) informs us that characteristics of the stimulus are critical, along with the perceiver, in determining a perception. Stimuli which are *moving, intense, new* or *unusual* are more likely to be noticed by a person.

A number of constancies are offered also by perceptual theorists. For instance, shape, size and color emerge as constants once the person is familiar with the object. The light shed on the object along with the position of the item might change but the person viewing it would recognize it based on his experience and familiarity with it.

Depth perception is quite obviously critical to reports offered by eyewitnesses to crimes. Although the retina is two-dimensional, the fact that one views objects with two eyes is important to our obtaining a three-dimensional effect. The process is more involved than that, however, and the individual draws on various cues—*monocular* and *binocular*—in structuring an image. Monocular cues include linear perspective, clearness, texture, interposition, movement and shadows (Morgan, 1974). That is to say, a single eye (monocular) is capable of distinguishing the above-mentioned characteristics of the object. Binocular cues, which rely on both eyes, are also relied upon in perception. They would include angles or *retinal disparity*. The experience is illustrated in the use of stereoscopic viewing devices. Simply stated, the fact that one eye is located in a different position from the other eye allows for the three-dimensional effect. Our field of vision is also expanded with two eyes. Exactly how this process works is uncertain, but information from both eyes is processed in the brain and a single perception results (Hilgard, Atkinson and Atkinson, 1975).

Perception psychologists sometimes talk about *hypothesis testing* in regard to the perceptions human beings construct. This is linked to the active role of the perceiver. The active nature of perception is pointed out in a study by Bruner and Potter (1964). These researchers found that in presenting a decreasing series of blurred slides to subjects, if an individual mistakenly claimed he recognized the object, he often was unable to identify it correctly until it became quite clear, clearer than would have been neces-

sary if it had been identified accurately originally. This suggests
that when a person once forms a perception based on his initial
viewing of an object, it becomes difficult to shake him from it.

Like many other theorists of human behavior, perceptual
psychologists do not agree on the dominance of *heredity* or *environment* in explaining the underlying nature of perception.
Some have cast this argument in terms of the *nativist* vs. the
empiricist point of view. While this question has implications for
theory and research, it is of less interest to those of us concerned
with the *functional* aspects of perception. In other words, legal
psychology is concerned with the accuracy and credibility of eyewitness testimony, but whether the quality of a given individual's
perception is the result of the learning that has occurred in his
environment or from his genetic endowment is relatively unimportant. *The question, quite simply, is what did he see and how
well did he see it.* Most psychologists now seem to agree that these
processes merge and that research investigations have yet to make
clear which area is more influential—heredity or environment.

Social Psychological Aspects

In applying the *functional* perspective to an analysis of an eyewitness account, the *selectivity* of perception looms as important.
Basically, the question is: why is it that with the massive bombard-
ment of stimuli to which the individual is exposed, he selects
certain portions to attend to? Somehow, the brain instructs us to
focus on certain events and ignore others. Some evidence suggests
that certain information, which apparently occurs unnoticed to
the individual, is suddenly brought into awareness. Hilgard,
Atkinson and Atkinson (1975) offer the example of the cocktail
party conversation in which a person picks up his name being
mentioned in a different conversation on the other side of the
room. The authors suggest that the nervous system apparently
monitors the other voices for relevant stimuli.

Experiments designed to study this phenomenon have been
conducted in which a person is exposed to two sets of auditory
stimuli, one in each ear, and then the person is questioned as to
what he heard or understood. Studies of this type appear to have
documented more thoroughly the existence of this everyday occur-

rence without yet illuminating the brain mechanism(s) responsible.

Bruner's (1973) work on the social psychology of perception is relevant here. In an early experiment which helped to establish the "New Look" approach to perceptual psychology, Bruner and Goodman (1947) examined the way in which *needs* influenced the perception of objects. The authors identified two types of perceptual determinants, *autochthonous* and *behavioral*. In the first instance, the highly predictable properties of the nervous system were included (phenomena discussed earlier in this chapter) pairing of information, closure, contrasting, size and color constancy, etc. The authors point out that given ideal viewing conditions, people respond in fixed, expected ways. However, when *behavioral* determinants are introduced, variations in perception begin to emerge. Bruner and Goodman (1947) included various adaptive functions such as emotional defense mechanisms (repression), the operation of temperamental characteristics such as introversion-extroversion motivation, learning, and social needs and values. These students of perception summarized this point of view by stating: "The organism exists in a world of more or less ambiguously organized stimuli. What the organism sees, what is *actually there* perceptually, represents some sort of compromise between what is presented by autochthonous processes and what is selected by behavioral ones" (p. 36).

In this early experiment, Bruner and Goodman (1947) found a relationship between the economic background ("rich" or "poor") of the children, who served as subjects, and their perceptions of discs. Seemingly, the study demonstrated that objects which were of value to the perceiver were accentuated in size (coins were accentuated while disks of equivalent size were not) and that this relationship was greater for children of poor economic background compared with wealthier youngsters. While the study has been criticized for methodological weaknesses, subsequent research efforts designed to explore the same basic type of phenomena have met with mixed results.

While initially the research findings of Levine, Chein and Murphy (1942) suggested that the *amount* of need was critical in shaping perception, subsequent research on needs has demonstrated that the *mode of striving* is more critical (Bruner, 1958).

In the original Levine, Chein, and Murphy (1942) study, sub-jects were shown a set of food pictures behind a screen that made them appear vague or ambiguous. Inquiry was directed at the subjects in terms of what they saw. The results indicated that as deprivation increased, up to the point of twelve hours, subjects demonstrated an increase in the number of food and eating re-sponses. After twelve hours, a reduction in food and eating re-sponses occurred. The authors sought to explain their findings in terms of different psychological mechanisms, but scholars today question their interpretations and methodology.

Linked to the early studies on needs was the work of Postman, Bruner, and McGinnies (1948) on personal values. In their study, the authors found that the speed and ease with which words were recognized when presented briefly in a perceptual apparatus (tachistoscope), were related to the value areas these words sym-bolized. The more dominating a particular value, the more quick-ly a person would identify words in that area.

In addition to having created interest in the role of *needs* in perceptual research, Bruner (1957) offered a second major con-tribution in his work on perceptual *readiness*. As part of this work, he started with the notion that perception involves an "act of categorization." This is a cognitive process in which the in-dividual uses cues to conceptualize and organize the stimuli he is exposed to. In an earlier paper entitled "Emotional Selectivity in Perception and Reaction," Bruner and Postman (1947) examined blockage in the perception of threatening words, and a later paper by McGinnies (1949) studied the raising of identification thresh-olds for taboo words. Out of this research, Bruner developed the concept of perceptual defense.

In summarizing his own research, along with that of colleagues, in the areas of *need* and *readiness*, Bruner (1958) commented: "Perceptual readiness, the ease with which items are recognized under less than optimal viewing conditions, seems to reflect not only the needs and modes of striving of a person but also to re-flect the requirement that surprise be minimized—that perceptual readiness be predictive in the sense of being tuned to what is likely to be present in the environment as well as what is needed for the pursuit of our enterprises." (p. 90) Bruner claimed that the anticipation of viewing an object was critical in the accuracy of perception and he noted that a train whistle prepared the person for seeing the train. In this respect, learning and previous experience were obviously important to his theory.

The implications of this research on the role of defensiveness in perception are significant for eyewitness testimony. One possible implication has to do with the distortion that may result from a person viewing a violent or otherwise "unacceptable" incident. Much like the impact of a taboo word, the "perceptual stress" of the scene may hinder accurate recognition. The person may even totally block out recognition. On the other hand, the witness's aroused interest might conceivably take the form of heightened visual acuity. Research generally on the effects of anxiety and tension on intellectual performance suggest that too little or too much reduces productivity while a moderate amount is beneficial.

In recent years, the "New Look" psychology has been criticized heavily. Erdelyi (1974), along with others, has taken this approach to task on a number of counts. A major criticism has been, "If perceptual defense is really perceptual, how can the perceiver selectively defend himself?" (p. 3). Another criticism, which points to the fact that the problem of what is perceptual bias may indeed be some type of cognitive response has been referred to as *response suppression.* This notion suggests that subjects recognize taboo words and neutral words equally well but are slower in verbalizing the embarrassing words and therefore longer response times ensue. Erdelyi (1974) has bypassed the problem of trying to determine at which point the bias injects itself by presenting a multisystem approach which views perceptual recognition as a continuous process. In his theory, bias may come into play during the initial perceiving of an object, but it may also present itself during the response process. There may be multiple points at which the integrity of the perceptual process as a whole breaks down. No single biasing effect invalidates another biasing effect.

The way in which personal relevance appears to be a factor in perception was evaluated by Jones and de Charms (1958). In two related experiments, the investigators set up situations in which a person (confederate) failed to meet the announced expectations or norms on a series of tasks. When his performance was linked to that of other group members, he was seen as less likeable along with being less dependable by these participants.

Conformity and Expectations

A different line of social psychological research that has ramifications for perception is that offered by Asch (1955) and his colleagues. Asch found that when groups of individuals were asked to state openly their observations on the lengths of various lines, many of the research subjects chose to conform to group opinion rather than adhere to what their sense perceptions told them. Confederates of the researchers participated in the series of experiments and contributed to "stacking the deck" against the subjects. Under normal conditions, individuals erred less than 1 percent of the time in their analysis of the lengths of various lines, but while under group pressure, the subjects swung over to the trumped up majority's opinion by 36.8 percent of the time. One quarter (25%) of the subjects, however, remained independent and never agreed with the phony premise of the majority.

In describing the individuals who succumbed to group pressure, Asch (1955) noted that a portion of that group yielded quickly and in effect stated, "I am wrong, they are right." Some claimed to have gone along so as to be helpful to the experimenter, but another group which was of greater concern to Asch "construed their difference from the majority as a sign of some general deficiency in themselves, which at all costs they must hide." (p. 33). They eagerly sought to merge with the majority, not being aware of the broader implications of their act. Most of the conforming subjects, Asch informs us, *underestimated* the frequency with which they bowed to group pressure.

The implications of this work for eyewitness identifications are obvious in at least one respect. Lineups in which more than one witness is present and in which the opportunity to confer with others exists may be riddled with error. More generally, of course, one might expect that the pressure—at times direct and at times subtle—on a prosecution witness to "give the police what they want" might be all too often the "clincher" in a case of disputed identity. This desire to perform in an expected fashion, in the case of eyewitnesses, has been documented by Buckhout (1974), and will be discussed at length later in this chapter. Rosenthal (1966), in particular, has described the critical way in which *expectation* generally seems to distort and bias research studies. In one study, a test administrator succeeded in obtaining the desired response by smiling at the subjects during their participation. In another investigation (Rosenthal, 1966) individuals were asked to select a certain face from a series of photographs. The research offered clues to the research assistants who administered the experiment, and this information somehow became translated into the experimental procedure. The results supported the general theory that the researcher's bias can be critical in affecting the outcome. Buckhout (1965) demonstrated that "the need for social approval" is important in understanding the individuals' performances in research. In his study, those high in need for social approval showed more attitude change than those low in need for social approval and control group subjects. A different side of the coin is discussed by Orne (1961) in analyzing the subject who becomes acutely aware of the researcher's intention. This may lead the subject to bend over backward "to be honest in his responses," thus countering the experimenter's preference with the result of biasing in the opposite direction. Once again, the implications for police behavior vis-à-vis participation in criminal prosecutions is self-evident.

In one of the classic cases of mistaken identity reported by Brochard (1932), *expectation* played a critical role. Both James Keeton and Judson Powers, who resided in Washington, D.C., were victims of a vicious attack at around midnight on September 20, 1922. Previous enmity had developed between the two victims and several members of the local electrical workers union, including Robert Sisson, Maurice Sullivan, and Earle Dean. Sisson and Sullivan had sought admission to the union, but just prior to their applications being processed, a strike broke out. Much to the dismay of the union members, the two victims had continued to work through the strike period. Notwithstanding the fact that the three accused assailants were able to offer alibis (principally from family members) for their activities on the night of September 20, all were convicted and sentenced. One had been identified from a photograph and a second was recognized as a foreman at the railway station where they were employed.

After being incarcerated for over one year and a half, Dean confessed to his participation along with naming seven different men. One of the actual assailants, a man named Smith, did look like Sisson. Dean, of course, had been correctly identified and had been observed at a restaurant a short time before the attack by Keeton. Keeton's mistaken identification of Sisson and Sullivan, however, appeared to have been linked directly to his previous experiences with these members of the electrical workers union. The jury, like the two victims, felt Sisson and Sullivan were guilty because of their strike activities and the suspicion that they had been vindictive toward what they had perceived as strike-breaking activity.

A more recent example of mistaken identity, which claimed the attention of readers throughout North America, was reported in the *Edmonton Journal* (1979). Reverend Bernard Pagano, a Roman Catholic priest, had been accused of a series of armed robberies in the Delaware area. A group of *seven* witnesses had identified him. During the course of Pagano's trial, Ronald Clouser stepped forward and confessed to the robberies, claiming that he had become desperate for money after a recent divorce battle. He also stated that he felt guilty about the priest's plight. Sensing that he was the only person who could exonerate him, he decided to confess.

Authoritarianism

Rokeach's (1960) work, *The Open and Closed Mind,* has paved the way for many additional studies on dogmatism and authoritarianism, including some on perception. One study in which authoritarianism of subjects was linked to perception was conducted by Shrauger and Altrocchi (1964). The perception of a status person was related to the needs of the perceiver. Authoritarians were more favorably disposed toward individuals who were at their level—a type of colleague or peer relationship—while their dogmatism appeared to interfere with their acceptance of strangers. The problem of ambiguity and an unstructured stimulus has been noted in the literature in relation to the authoritarian personality.

Related studies on ethnic identification have yielded some interesting results. Siegel (1954) offered his research subjects opportunities to assign ethnic labels to twenty photographs of Mexicans. The subjects were able, also, to choose a nonethnic label. He found that there was a statistically significant relationship between individuals who scored high on authoritarianism and their choice of ethnicity. Scodel and Austrin (1957) also found that authoritarians among Jewish and nonJewish subjects were more apt to identify photographs as Jewish.

Stereotyping and Prejudice

Some psychological research has concerned itself with the irrational and prejudicial manner in which people are viewed. A study by Second, Bevan, and Katz (1956) found that prejudiced subjects, more than the nonprejudiced subjects, tended to exaggerate the difference between blacks and whites in skin color, a not-surprising finding.

Gordon Allport and Leo Postman (1958) reported on an interesting experiment in which rumor, in addition to perception, played a role. Subjects were shown slides of "semi-dramatic" pictures presenting a variety of details. One example was a picture of a subway train (apparently New York City) in which a number of people are seated and a black man is standing talking with a somewhat shorter white male dressed in working clothes. The shorter man has a razor in his left hand (lowered at his side), while his right hand is pointing in the face of the black man. One typical response offered to this scene involves a subject's description that "This is a subway train in New York headed for Portland Street. There is a Jewish woman and a Negro who has a razor in his hand. The woman has a baby or a dog. The train is going to Deyer Street , and nothing much happened" (p. 57) . This type of distortion on the part of research subjects—an apparent reflection of stereotyping and prejudice—was not uncommon. Some subjects were asked to describe the pictures to others who had not seen them, and they passed on (rumor) their misunderstandings in the process.

Based on their findings, the researchers developed a three-pronged theory which included *leveling, sharpening,* and *assimila-*

tion. Leveling referred to the process whereby as rumor travels, it tends to grow shorter, more concise, more easily grasped and told. In successive versions, fewer words are used and fewer details are mentioned. *Sharpening* occurred in a reciprocal relationship with leveling. It was the selective perception, retention, and reporting of a limited number of details from a larger context. The third aspect of the rumor transmission process was defined as *assimilation. Assimilation* accounted for the transpositions, importations, and other falsifications. It had to do with the attraction exerted upon rumor by habits, interests and fantasies in the receiver's mind. The authors noted assimilation could be identified by the way in which material becomes woven into a story. Initially, items are sharpened or leveled to fit the principal idea of the story, and then new material may be added to round out the story and make it more coherent.

In Borchard's (1932) classic work entitled *Convicting The Innocent,* he discussed the variety of motives and emotions that affect witnesses' accounts:

> Into the identification enter other motives, not necessarily stimulated originally by the accused personality—the desire to requite a crime, to exact vengeance upon the person believed guilty, to find a scapegoat, to support, consciously or unconsciously, an identification already made by another. Thus, doubts are resolved against the accused. How valueless are these identifications by the victim of a crime is indicated by the fact that in eight of these cases the wrongfully accused person and the really guilty bore not the slightest resemblance to each other, whereas in twelve other cases, the resemblance, while fair, was not at all close. In only two cases can the resemblance by called striking. (p. xiii)

MEMORY

As Marshall (1963) has observed, in the context of the courtroom one of the chief objectives of the cross-examination is to demonstrate the weaknesses of memory in a particular witness. Memory, much like perception, remains poorly understood. Psychologists, neurologists and others are just beginning to develop a sketchy understanding of these processes.

While the theoretical underpinnings of memory are of interest, the focus of legal psychology is on the functional aspects. Regardless of the particular brain functions that contribute to a person's ability to recall information, the issues raised in a criminal proceeding are "situation specific." What does individual "X" recall about the night of January 9, one month ago? How detailed and clear is *he* about the events of that evening, and how does *he* perform under the stress of cross-examination? The use of lie detection devices, while restricted in many jurisdictions, are more commonplace today than ever before, particularly in law enforcement and industrial settings. They are frequently used to test the veracity of a person's statement about events in the past. While our knowledge of memory processes is very incomplete and scientists are unable to make precise predictions about a person's ability to recall, it is nonetheless of value to review the current state of the art.

Historically, psychologists were more interested in exploring the relationship of learning to memory than they are today. The shift has been in the direction of studying memory itself. Murdock (1973) has provided a basic outline of the stages and processes of memory. He describes three basic stages as follows:

Encoding involves the basic registration of information. When you view a painting, meet a person for the first time, or observe a particular event, the information is temporarily registered or encoded through the operation of sensory receptors and internal nervous circuits.

Storage, still not well understood, is the aspect of the process that stores information. Whether it is an active or passive process is of interest to memory psychologists.

Retrieval, as suggested by the term, concerns itself with the accessibility of information. If a witness is asked about certain events that took place three years earlier, will that person be able to get access to that information, assuming that the first two stages of the process operated effectively?

As Murdock (1974) points out, not being able to recall some information is not helpful in providing any clues as to where the problem lies: encoding, storage, or retrieval.

Hilgard, Atkinson, and Atkinson (1975) have outlined four types of remembering: *redintegrative memory, recall, recognition,* and *relearning.* Briefly they are defined as follows: *Redintegrative* is a form of memory (recollection) that refers to the reintegration or reestablishment of an earlier experience on the basis of partial cues. The stimuli to redintegrate are like souvenirs or reminders of a distant past. A particular object may come to mind that allows the person to remember all or parts of a particular experience. This type of remembering has implications for eyewitness testimony.

Recall as defined by psychologists is most easily tested in the laboratory (Hilgard, Atkinsons and Atkinson, 1975). One demonstrates that present performance is different from what it would have been if there were no residue from the past. An experimenter can demonstrate that one remembers how to drive a car by getting in and driving away (regardless of the fact that the person has not driven for a year).

Recognition is the type of remembering, of course, most crucial to eyewitness testimony. It does not appear to be a process well understood by scientific psychology. Nonetheless, its occurrences are extremely common in our everyday experiences. We may not be able to know precisely how or in what circumstance we have known a person, but we are sure we have seen this person before. Recognition is tested in the laboratory setting, for example, by exposing a person to a series of photographs. The person is then asked to identify them, at a later point, after they have been mixed in with some other photographs. In testing for memory, Murdock (1973) views a recognition process as involving some sort of *comparison,* while recall requires a *search.*

Relearning is a form of remembering that can be illustrated by asking a person to learn material that was once learned before. Even though certain information may seem to have been forgotten completely, by demonstrating that it can be learned more quickly on the second occasion, evidence is provided for the fact that a residue of the previous learning existed.

Another important issue for psychologists interested in memory is the nature of forgetting. One theory that has considerable support and is perhaps the most straightforward is *decay through disuse* (Hilgard, Atkinson and Atkinson, 1975). Simply stated, it is the idea that learning leaves a trace in the brain, and that over a period of time the normal metabolic processes cause a fading or decay of the memory. Some retention continues over extended periods of time, however, even without so-called "practice" or "reinforcement," and this phenomenon is not easily explained by a simple decay theory. A different problem is posed by the senile person; that individual has trouble remembering events in the immediate past, but can provide detailed accounts from his or her much earlier adolescent years.

Interference Effects is a second theory of forgetting that explains memory loss on the basis of the person learning other information in between the time of his exposure to the original material and his test on that material. Adams (1967) described this approach as "certain classes of responses occurring before the acquisition of criterion responses to be tested later for retention, or between acquisition and test, cause a decrement in criterion behavior. The decrement is the loss we call forgetting" (p. 51). A frequently cited example involves a group of research subjects who learn Task A, then Task B, to be followed by memory testing of Task A. A control group learns Task A but is not exposed to any intervening material and then is tested on Task A. Performances of the two groups are compared and inevitably the scores of subjects who were not exposed to the interfering effects (retroactive inhibition) perform in a superior fashion. A parallel problem of retention (proactive inhibition) has been noted when an experimental group learns Task A, then B, and is tested on B. Comparisons with control groups that were not exposed to Task A demonstrate that the prior learning reduced retention of the second, task, B.

Any consideration of forgetting, as Hilgard, Atkinson and Atkinson (1975) note, most take into account emotional and motivational factors. *Repression* certainly could, and unquestionably does, play a key role in the forgetting or blocking out of upsetting material or information eyewitnesses are exposed to. It is a psychoanalytic term that is rooted in Freud's work. Essentially, it involves an unconscious blotting out of a previous event. Psychoanalytically trained therapists believe that even though a person may not have conscious access to the material, the trauma of the original experience will nonetheless reflect itself in terms of neurotic impairment in the adult. The early experience may express itself in some disturbing way years later, thus the necessity for re-moving the blockage. Hypnotists have also been somewhat suc-cessful in removing the blockage to allow recall of the critical event. A key assumption of the hypnotist is that the relaxed state or trance frees up the person and thereby gives him access to his memory. Increasingly, one hears of law enforcement personnel drawing on hypnotists to assist in the interviewing of frightened witnesses.

A different line of research has been offered by Penfield (1952) in conjunction with his neurological surgery. He stimulated electrically certain areas of the brain during surgery on epileptic patients and found that some of them provided vivid, detailed ac-counts of early life experiences. This work provided clear evi-dence of the fact that the brain stores a great amount of detailed information.

The Two-Process Theory of Memory

I wish to complete this brief discussion of memory by focusing on a contemporary theory, the two-process theory, that integrates *short-term memory* and *long-term memory*. An example of short-term memory is illustrated by the request to repeat back a series of numbers on an intelligence test. Long-term memory might in-volve a request from an associate for the person's previous street address of five years before.

One viewpoint reported in Hilgard, Atkinson, and Atkinson (1975) presents short-term memory (STM) as decaying rapidly, while long-term memory (LTM) is seen as a more permanent storage system. Under long-term memory, recall is "cue" related in that upon presentation of a certain stimulus, the person is able to recall the particular item into awareness. This theory suggests that by "rehearsing" (repeating) information in short-term mem-ory, decay is avoided. Also, STM is of limited size, and unless in-formation is either rehearsed or placed in long-term storage, it fades away. Long-term storage is conceived of as being more permanent and unrestricted in size. Contemporary theorists ap-pear to find this approach appealing, because it explains most of the circumstances of forgetting, albeit in a crude fashion.

Hilgard, Atkinson and Atkinson (1975) state the two-process

theory provides several reasons why forgetting may occur:

> Immediate recall may fail because subsequent inputs to STM have caused the information to decay. Long-term recall may fail because the information was never transferred to LTM or because not enough cues are available at the time of attempted recall to locate the information in LTM.

Murdock (1973) notes that long-term memories are more vulnerable to the intrusion of other material or the interferences commented on earlier. On the other hand, short-term memory can fail on items that are difficult to discriminate on the basis of similarity of sound.

When one considers the problem posed by an eyewitness to a crime, who might have had a fleeting glimpse of a person's face one year earlier, given the fact that delays in the criminal justice system are often longer, the implications of the previous discussion become obvious.

A recently reported mugging in the *New York Times* (Brody, 1978) offers an example. Robert Brody was approached by a knife wielding mugger as he attempted to enter his apartment on July 5, 1975. The man relieved Brody of his money and after gaining entrance to the apartment, took off with various possessions, a television set, radio, clock, watch and suitcase. During this episode, the man assaulted Brody as he attempted to resist him. and Brody suffered some wounds that required hospital treatment.

Two weeks later, detectives assigned to the case showed Brody a black and white photograph and inquired if he were the "guy." When the victim confirmed that he was, a lineup was arranged in Manhattan at the Criminal Courts Building. The detectives were not there on the designated day as they were at a funeral. Another lineup was arranged and again cancelled because the defense attorney prevented the suspect from being released from prison, where he was being held for other crimes, until a judge authorized it. Several weeks passed and a third lineup was arranged but it, too, never materialized as corrections officials could not locate the offender at the Rikers Island institution. At about this time, the recovering victim observes, "Meanwhile, the pink scar on my chest is fading and my right lung is billowing freely. I see people in my neighborhood who resemble the suspect. At this point, I am not even sure the cops have the right guy."

Finally, the lineup is held and Brody is ushered into a room at the Criminal Courts Building, some four months after the knifing, where he observes six candidates through a one-way mirror. Quickly, he realizes that he does not recognize any of the six men. In this instance, memory had faded sufficiently in four months to the extent that identification was impossible, notwithstanding the fact that the original observation of the criminal took place in daytime over a period of several minutes and that a subsequent photographic identification seemingly "bolstered" the original perception.

In addition to possible *interference* effects, which can weaken long-term memory and very possibly did in Brody's case, there is always the question of the original *encoding*. Did the victim get a good look at the suspect and were other conditions such as lighting and time exposure adequate? While law enforcement personnel may present a photograph to the witness, either singly or as part of an array, this may or may not be sufficient enough to allow a positive identification at a later lineup, witness the Brody case. Furthermore, the presentation of a single photograph to a witness is potentially biasing and is apt to be ruled illegal in court (*Gilbert v. California,* 1967; *Moore v. Illinois,* 1977). Brody's remark regarding the confusion caused by seeing people on the street "who resemble the suspect," suggests that interference played a role in this case.

While a witness to a lineup is faced with a recognition type of task instead of a recall type of task (the latter considered to be much more difficult by students of memory), it is nonetheless a formidable undertaking if the original *encoding* was weak or if an extended time lapse allowed for *interference* effects. *Interference* is undoubtedly more destructive to the original perception if the images and perceptions that the person is exposed to subsequently are very similar to the original perceptual stimulus (Laughery, Fessler and Yoblick, 1974). In acknowledging the importance of stimulus cues in evoking a memory, they might be lacking totally or be minimally available in the viewing of a lineup. The original scene of the crime, which may have many cues embedded in it, would be different and the attire worn by the suspect would have changed in all probability at the time of the lineup. Lighting and sound variables might also play a role, as differences created by conditions of the lineup compared to the scene of the crime may hinder identification.

While the argument could be raised that these differences may help to protect the rights of the accused by making identification more difficult, the counterargument is that they unfairly change the condition of the original perception to the extent that they render ultimate identification exceedingly difficult.

Forbes (1975) found that exposure to a large number of face stimuli prior to the targets impaired subsequent recognition accuracy. Thus, he apparently demonstrated the effect of interference on facial recognition. A contrasting view was presented by Davies, Shepherd, and Ellis (1979). They arranged for four groups of fifteen subjects, aged twenty to sixty-five years of age, to observe a videotape of three men whom they were later asked to identify in a recognition test. One group of subjects, who searched through a sequence of 100 facial photos, were less accurate in identifying the targets than a control group who spent an equivalent amount of time listening to a comedy tape. Another group who rated the photos on attractiveness, not identity, demonstrated test performance similar to the control group. In interpreting their findings, however, the authors claim that a theory of *internal criterion* shift better explains their results than a straightforward explanation of interference effects in which simple exposure to mugshots has a weakening impact.

The emotional factor, particularly anxiety, needs to be considered in any determination of accuracy of recognition. The role of anxiety in eyewitness identification was included in a paper presented by Mueller (1978) at the American Psychological Association's Symposium on "Memory For Faces." Mueller found that anxious subjects did not do as well as less anxious subjects. He also noted that several experiments had shown this and that the finding may have been related to poorer *encoding* on the part of those whose performance was inferior. Mueller's (1978) interest was directed at what types of activity aid in recognition of facts rather than the more frequent experimental approach that seeks to identify characteristics of faces that affect recognition. He concluded his presentation by stating that *encoding* activities are important, perhaps as important as features of the face alone.

In the case of *Moore v. Illinois* (1977), Supreme Court Justice Blackmun, in a concurring opinion, argued that the face-to-face encounter between offender and victim undoubtedly resulted in an "indelible impression" being created in the victim's mind. Specifically, he stated:

> I disassociate myself from the implication twice appearing in the Court's opinion, *ante,* at 2 and, at 9—that there is something insignificant or unreliable about a rape victim's observation during the crime of the facial features of her assailant when that observation lasts "only 10 to 15 seconds." Time, of course, is always a comparative matter. Fifteen seconds perhaps would mean little in the identification of scores of separate individuals participating in an illegal riot. But 10 to 15 seconds of observation of the face of a rapist at midday by his female victim during the commission of the crime by no means is insufficient to leave an accurate and indelible impression on the victim. (p. 4054)

Justice Blackmun obviously does not envision the possibility that the emotional trauma of the rape might have interfered with the original perception or its later report. One would suspect that he would be unreceptive to a theory that a psychological defense mechanism such as *repression* could play a possible role in such an instance. For him, it is "common sense."

Factually, of course, the Supreme Court Justice appears to be ignorant of scientific evidence concerning perceptual and memory processes, including facial recognition; most of his fellow lawyers are in the same boat. Interestingly enough, the subject of facial recognition has received a good deal of attention from psychologists. It represents, also, an area of research investigation in which perception and memory processes converge.

RESEARCH ON FACIAL RECOGNITION

Some of the studies on facial recognition are not unrelated to the earlier discussed work on prejudice and stereotyping. One such study, by Malpass and Kravitz (1969), showed that people perceive more clearly members of their own race. White subjects never exceeded 79 percent correct recognition of white faces. Subjects had received a single brief exposure, and recognition was tested immediately afterward. Black subjects scored 67 percent for accuracy in identifying black faces under conditions of immediate recognition. In another widely cited study, Pettigrew, Allport and Barnett (1958) asked subjects to identify the racial membership of human faces presented in pairs. A certain amount of ambiguity was present. The authors attempted to include all the possible combinations of ethnic groups residing in South Africa. Findings indicated that Afrikaner subjects (Caucasians of Dutch ancestry) tended to identify the ambiguous composite faces belonging to either the "European" (white) or "African" (black) categories more often than other ethnic group subjects. The mixed physical shading of "Colored" or "Indian" were consequently less frequently chosen and has been cited as an example of the influence of racism in this highly segregated South African society. In a more recent study of racial factors in facial recognition (Chance, Goldstein and McBride, 1975), it was found that white subjects were better able to identify white faces than black faces or Japanese faces. Blacks were better able to discern their own race faces followed by white faces and then Japanese faces. The researchers suggested that the differences appeared to be related to the subjects' past experiences with various kinds of faces. In a general way, Goldstein (1977) has stated that when individuals are given single, limited exposure to faces in experimental situations, an average error of 30 percent can be expected and that rarely will the average drop below 15 percent.

Finally, in a doctoral dissertation completed at Ohio State University, Linda James (1976) studied "Differential Face Recognition and Stereotyped Perception." Using faces which depicted various combinations of characteristics from Caucasoid to Negroid, she found that as faces displayed more Negroid characteristics, they were more difficult for white subjects to discriminate among. Also, black subjects were able to recognize faces more accurately than white subjects. In summarizing her findings, she states, "The results of this experiment support the idea that culture does influence perception."

The idea that occupational labels might differentially influence the perception of photographs was investigated by Secord, Bevan and Dukes (1953). Subjects viewed six photographs with six occupational labels in different combinations and then they filled out a personality rating scale for each labeled photograph. No support was found for the major hypothesis of the study—namely, there was no evidence that occupational stereotypes distorted the perceptions of the pictures. Substantial evidence of the existence of occupational stereotypes and of physionomic stereotypes was found, however, the former by presenting occupations without photographs to one group, and the latter by showing photographs without occupational labels to a second group. In short, ratings seemed to be determined largely by the perception of photographs independent of the labels.

In identifying a person's face, are age of the subject or age of stimulus face factors? Goldstein and Chance (1964) attempted to answer this question for youthful subjects by asking groups of kindergarten, third- and eighth-grade students. Consistent with an earlier study's findings (Brooks and Goldstein, 1963), the authors found that older children are better able to recognize faces than younger children. All subjects were given a brief exposure to a series of photographs and then were asked to pick them out from other pictures included for background a short time later. The two experiments conducted by the researchers offered mixed findings, however, concerning the question of the ease with which older faces are identified. On this question they interpreted their data to mean that given a large number of faces from young, middle and old categories, there will be no consistent relationship between age of face and identification.

In an attempt to compare the ease of recognition of faces with other material, Goldstein and Chance (1970) contrasted responses to faces with those to snow crystals and ink blots. Accuracy scores were clearly superior for faces (71%), followed by ink blots (46%) and then snow crystals (33%). An incidental finding was that women were better able to recognize faces than men. More recent work provides further confirmation of this finding.

Yarmy (1978) undertook a study of recognition memory for male and female faces. He commented on the fact, during his presentation of his study at the American Psychological Association Convention, that results of previous research on sex differences in memory for faces was mixed, but that females seemed to have a slight advantage over males in their ability in this area. In his work, Yarmy found that women were generally superior to men in their ability to recognize faces. Concerning the characteristics and sex of the faces remembered, he stated that the results added strong support to the notion that "what is remembered are faces that are attractive and likeable if female."

In attempting to explain why women are superior to men in facial recognition tasks, he advanced the notion that women learn early more than men that attractiveness is important while men learn strength and power are important. Finally, in an unusual experiment, Yarmy sought to explore the role of the self in memory for faces, including the image one has of one's own face. Subjects were asked to rate different photographs of themselves along dimensions of *intelligence, sociableness, trustworthiness,* etc. One of the key findings from this experimental work was that females were superior to males in recognizing their own faces, particularly for those faces labeled as *sociable.*

In his concluding remarks, Yarmy noted that the performance differences between men and women might not be important for the courts as "we're not ready to go into court as expert witnesses and say women are better than men." Offered as a footnote to his work, he stated that subjects' confidence was not related to accuracy of recognition in his research.

Goldstein's (1978) paper presented at the American Psychological Association's Symposium on "Memory For Faces" focused on intraindividual consistency in visual recognition memory. He noted that some literature on eyewitness testimony suggests that the ability to recognize faces is a *skill* and if so, perhaps it is possible to distinguish between individuals who are good at it from those who are not by employing a "morning after test for face recognition." That is to say, perhaps the courts could give a test to a witness who had claimed to observe the face of a suspect to determine the probability of whether or not his identification was accurate.

Goldstein arranged an experimental situation in which subjects were tested over three sessions. In addition, they were asked to remember the person as different poses of the face were shown for the *study* and *trial* sessions. They were thus informed that the same photograph or pose would not be repeated. The purpose was to measure the consistency with which subjects were able to recognize the forty-eight "targets" that were mixed in with "decoys." *The results demonstrated that womens' performance, consistent with Yarmy's (1978) findings, was superior to men on facial recognition.* In all three comparison days, men were more consistent in errors committed. However, the researcher noted that while intra-individual behavior is more consistent than "hit" behavior, we are a long way away from being able to use these data in the courtroom.

Goldstein advances a logical extension of his findings in stating that "women pay more attention to nonverbal stimuli." On the important question of consistency of face recognition, however, the findings were not encouraging for a "morning after test." Goldstein (1978) reported that consistency of face recognition was too weak to predict future recognition.

The factors of *delay* along with *similarity* in the recognition of faces have direct implications for the criminal justice system, as sometimes witnesses are asked to make identifications in a lineup or in court after extended delays, as was noted earlier in Brody (1978). Several recent studies bear on this issue. Laughery, along with Alexander and Lane (1971) contrived an experimental situation designed to resemble the experience witnesses are confronted with in criminal cases. Among other things, their findings indicated that "target position" was a critical factor in recognition—recognition accuracy decreased as the number of decoy pictures preceding the target increased. In a follow-up study, Laughery, Fessler, Lenorovitz and Yoblick (1974) sought clarification of issues raised in the earlier work along with investigation of new problems involving identification of faces. The researchers found no differences in subjects' ability to pick out faces in the one-week delay period when compared with the four-minute delay sequence. Slides and motion picture film were used in the presentation of faces to different groups of subjects, and the recognition through use of slides proved superior. The authors point out that in studies involving word recognition, decrements in performance have been demonstrated consistently over time and that the lack of differences in their study on facial recognition was surprising.

In this experiment, subjects picked out "targets" from among 149 "decoys."

In a second series of experiments, the authors examined the issue of facial *similarity* and its relationship to discrimination ability. All three experiments (in this second phase) demonstrated that the *similarity* of the "decoys" to the "target" proved to be an extremely important factor in the ability of subjects to successfully identify the correct face. In fact, these investigators claim that the similarity between the decoys and targets was more critical than the number of decoys. They also suggest the possibility of moving away from "linear" searches during criminal investigations and toward "interactive" searches. The latter would consist of a procedure in which the witness would give feedback to the administrator of the photographic display in terms of differences and similarities between the suspect and the facial pictures presented. This process resembles the one used by police artists in their composite drawings of criminal suspects.

The question of *similarity* of appearance raised itself for the author after recently observing a lineup conducted at the Manhattan District Attorney's office in New York City. This lineup was conducted by a young Assistant District Attorney who was investigating a case in which a Russian, Alexander Makarovsky, was alleged to have set off an explosion at the offices of a Russian newspaper, the *New Russian Word*. Some details were presented in a story in the *New York Post* (1978). The suspect entered with his attorney and was given the choice of determining his position in the lineup along with his identification number. He was free to change either/both after each of three witnesses separately viewed the lineup through a one-way mirror.

A makeup expert, formerly with N.B.C. Television in New York City, was brought in to make up the other lineup participants, as the suspect had a mustache as well as a beard. The author was informed that this was unusual and it may have occurred in response to a request from defense counsel. The six lineup stand-ins (decoys) were all New York City police officers, only two of whom were bearded and mustachioed. The others were "made up" by the expert. The lineup decoys then, while not actually resembling the suspect in terms of facial features, were not sufficiently different in appearance to focus undue attention on the suspect. For instance, the suspect's right cheek appeared to be redder than his left cheek, and when defense counsel brought this to the attention of the lineup administrator, the makeup man was then instructed to redden the cheeks of other lineup participants.

The question of just how far authorities should go to select or "make up" decoys to resemble the suspect is not adequately addressed in any of the U.S. Supreme Court opinions on eyewitness testimony. As the experimental work of Laughery, Fessler, Lenorovitz and Yoblick (1974) has demonstrated, similarity, as common sense would suggest, is a powerful factor that influences ability to pick the target person. As one increases similarity, one reduces accuracy of identification, and this in turn serves to assist the accused.

Of the three witnesses who separately observed the lineup which included Makarovsky, only one made a tentative identification. She had observed him from a window located approximately sixty feet from above the point of his exit from the building in which the explosion occurred. In response to the question, "Do you recognize anyone?" she had responded, "Maybe Number Five but I don't remember the beard." It is debatable as to whether or not such a weak identification has any value. While the original viewing took place at approximately 3:30 A.M., the high intensity lights situated at W. 56th Street in New York City provided bright illumination in the area.

There is evidence that stereotypes of criminals may be a factor in judgments of guilt or innocence. Shoemaker, South and Lowe (1973) studied responses of college subjects to a series of photographs of middle-aged white males. Photographs were then presented to groups of subjects under three experimental conditions. The authors found that not only was there a general consensus (good-bad) or criminal-noncriminal stereotype but also a stereotype for each specific type of offense. Both negative and positive stereotypes appeared to exist for the crimes of homosexuality, murder, robbery and treason. These stereotypes correlated with judgments of guilt or innocence, and males exercised these stereotypical judgments to a greater degree than females. The implications drawn from this research included:

(1) Because "mug shots" resemble the photographs employed in this study, questions concerning witness identification of suspects when using photos arises. The authors suggest that this type of distortion may introduce itself in cases where the witness did have a good, clear look at the suspect.
(2) Witnesses to crimes may be influenced in their judgments of the offender by the images (stereotypes) of what a particular type of criminal generally looks like.

Among the different characteristics of faces studied by social psychologists is attractiveness (Shepherd and Ellis, 1973). In one study, subjects were better able to recognize women's faces judged either high or low on attractiveness than those judged moderate. The time span between initial exposure and recognition testing varied between the immediate posttest period, six days, and thirty-five days. Conventional wisdom has it that some faces are unforgettable and this research appears to provide some support for that notion. As the authors comment, some faces may possess unique characteristics rendering them memorable.

Goldstein, Stephenson and Chance (1977) explored the theme of why some faces are more memorable than others in a series of experiments. They studied the responses of white college students to mixed racial (black and white) photo arrays. After the *target* photos were initially presented, they were later placed in arrays with *distractor* (new) photos to test recognition. Results indicated that some faces of distractors were picked more often than others, and some were never mistaken as targets. Results were statistically significant at the .05 level of confidence. The authors suggested that the reasons for this phenomenon were very unclear, although they suspect that some distractors have an "everyman" quality. Perhaps some distractors possessed one, two, or even more characteristics that are similar to many other faces in the general population.

The implications for lineups are obvious. If a witness is unsure of the suspect, he may be more apt to identify a decoy (distractor) if that individual is of the type that was more frequently picked in the above-mentioned study. Consistent with this outcome, the rights of the accused would be afforded further protection given the vulnerability of false identifications of other lineup participants. At this point, however, not nearly enough is known about this aspect of the process of misidentification to suggest a remedy to police and court personnel.

Struad and Mueller's (1977) work was concerned with the question of the depth of analysis of faces and subsequent recognition. They hypothesized that individuals who make more searching analyses ("deep") of faces will demonstrate better recognition than those who engage in casual ("shallow") analysis. Their study was an outgrowth of Bower and Karlin's (1974) work, "Depth of Processing of Pictures of Faces and Recognition Memory." In the "deep" processing, subjects were asked to make judgments of honesty, while in the "shallow" condition, they were merely required to identify the sex of the person. A slide projector was used in the experiment to flash pictures of male and female subjects onto a screen for brief intervals. Findings indicated that "deep" processing led to superior recognition memory.

In perhaps the largest cross-sectional study of facial recognition, Bahrick, Bahrick and Wittlinger (1975) studied 392 high school graduates' recognition of classmates. The retention interval varied from two weeks to fifty-seven years and included classes of various sizes. As the authors point out, the advantage of supplementing laboratory research with this type of investigation, in which statistical adjustments are exchanged for the experimental control of the laboratory, is that an extended time period can be examined. The findings of this study indicate that information is preserved over much longer periods of time than has been demonstrated in laboratory research. The effect of practice (reinforcement) and overlearning are cited as reasons for the fact that subjects *recognized* and matched names and faces for several hundred classmates but could *recall* only a small number. Recall was uncorrelated with class size of recognition performance. The investigators point out that the findings support a theory of memory in which "generative and retrieval processes are independent of storage processes." Also, the *social context* was critical in the ability of subjects to *recall* information. It served as a vehicle for subjects, apparently providing cues to the identity of classmates. Once this connecting link was lost, the *recall* process failed but *recognition* was still possible.

In recent years, police departments have relied frequently upon composite sketches and photographs of suspects who were being sought. Typically, a single witness or series of witnesses provide information concerning the facial features of the suspect and a police artist composes a drawing based on this information. It is then shown to the witnesses, and various modifications are sketched in, based on the "feedback" given to the artist. The sketch is then published in newspapers, shown on television, or circulated in selected areas, e.g. pawn shops. The approach remains controversial as it is not clear how successful a technique it is in the apprehension of individuals sought by law enforcement officers. Instances of mistaken identity may arise occasionally as the Barry Moskowitz case illustrates (Raab, 1978), or the dissimilarity between the composite face and the actual person becomes ultimately dramatically revealed. The notorious "Son of Sam" case, in which sketches of the then unknown David Berkowitz were circulated, is an example of the disparity that may emerge between an artist's drawing and the actual person. In this instance, however, the artist probably had very weak information on which to work. If the drawing does not closely resemble the person sought, does the published sketch hinder the apprehension of the suspect?

In a discussion which I held with New York City police personnel associated with the "Artist Unit," I became aware of the fact that their major concern was focused around the interviews they conducted with witnesses. The critical aspect for them became the question of how good was the witness. The witness' value was related to both the strength of the original observation and the ability to report this information. In short, the issues for the police artist are very similar to those posed by other eyewitness identifications, but the information must be elicited in an interview sometimes with the aid of photographs.

One member of the unit mentioned that he categorized all witnesses into categories of *active* or *passive*. The active witness freely contributes what he knows, and this aids the artist in gauging the credibility of the person. Usually this type of witness offers greater information. The passive witness is "very difficult," according to this artist, and he mentioned the problem posed by the temptation to "lead" such a person. By definition, the passive witness offers minimal information and the burden shifts to the interviewer to elicit what he knows. Notwithstanding the problems involved, this unit appears to have achieved some remarkable successes in assisting various New York City detectives and investigators. The validity of this statement is borne out when artist sketches are compared with photographs of the ultimately convicted offenders. It must be acknowledged, however, that it is possible that a sketch may have contributed to a later misidentification. The witness may unwittingly rely on the sketch rather than the original observation as the basis for making a later corporeal identification. Finally, it was pointed out by some of the artists that "our aim is to come up with a *type* [author's italics] to try to stimulate a person's mind." It was their view that for the most part, to expect a close *resemblance* between the drawing and the actual person was to expect too much from the process.

Social psychological researchers are becoming interested in this problem and a very recent study by Davies, Ellis, and Shepherd (1978) sheds some light on the value of facial drawings. Two experiments were conducted. In the first study, three groups of college students (twenty-seven each) were asked to identify well-known faces presented either as photographs, detailed line drawings, or outline drawings. The main finding was that the percentage correct increased geometrically as a function of the detail present. That is to say, photographs were identified accurately more than "line" drawings, which in turn were more frequently identified than "line outlines." Average ratings for ten target faces were 8.98 (photographs), 4.68 (line drawings), and only 2.35 (line outlines). As revealed in these figures, even the more detailed sketches or line drawings of well-known people were identified accurately less than 50 percent of the time. Clearly, line drawings—detailed or bare outlines—are very inferior to photographs in eliciting accurate identifications. Even well-known persons frequently escaped recognition when their three-quarter profiles were drawn and presented to college students.

A second experiment was designed to explore the importance of facial pose in recognition. Subjects were exposed to "full face" photos or drawings, while other subjects viewed either "three-quarter" profiles of photos or drawings. The research design also allowed for manipulation of the "pose" variable: to what extent might identification be hindered as a result of initially viewing a subject's face in one pose but then being asked to recognize the same face later in a different pose?

Results indicated that changing the pose of the stimulus face from the initial exposure to the later test period had no significant impact on recognition levels. "Full face" presentations were not significantly different than "three-quarters profile" presentations in terms of identifications. As the researchers note, the practical implications of the last finding do not suggest that there is any value in having police personnel prepare three-quarter profile shots of suspects versus traditional "full face" mug shots. Finally, the authors speculate that the "shading and depth cues" offered by the photographs seemed to be important ingredients in assisting the subjects in the recognition tasks.

Lane (1972) in a study of "best possible position" found that "there is no statistically best pose position for identifying human faces from pictures, although the front position tends to be better than profile of either of the two portraits. The assumption that the portrait pose contains more information useful to the witness cannot be supported. It is difficult at this point to say anything definite about the information contained in the different pose positions since it is always possible that S's use different kinds of information as a result of seeing the different poses" (p. 34).

Finally, Laughery (1978) recently reported on a research investigation that was designed to compare artists' sketches with so-called "Identi-kit" constructions of faces. The Identi-kit is a device which includes standard facial features—mouths, ears, eyes, noses, chins, etc.—and based on information provided by a witness, the technician tries to construct a likeness of the suspect. Police departments use them.

College subjects were brought into the psychological laboratory and then exposed to a target person. There were ninety-seven white male targets employed along with 182 witnesses. Three

police artists, along with three technicians (using Identi-kits) provided the stimuli for different subjects. Initially, witnesses came
to a room and completed a data form and they then were told that
they would see a target and later be assigned to work with a
technician or artist. Discussions of between seven or eight
minutes were then scheduled with artists or technicians. In trying
to cope with the problem of "how do you quantify the goodness of
fit or likeness," Laughery (1978) relied upon a six-point scale and
asked people to make judgments about goodness of fit. An additional variable included in the research was the factor of *view* vs.
description. *View* involved the process of relating information to
artists or technicians (Identi-kit) as the stimulus was being observed, while *description* required the subject to provide information from memory of the target.

In general, artists' sketches were superior to technicians' constructions from Identi-kits. Also, not surprisingly, productions
from *view* were superior to those from *descriptions*. Some artists
or technicians did generate better images than others. Interestingly enough, the experience of personnel (either artists or technicians) was not a significant factor. Also, quality of sketches or
Idenit-kit composites was not related to how long the witnesses
took to generate the images.

Laughery (1978) concludes that the Identi-kit does not have
the variety of materials to draw on. As he stated, "There are times
when the right nose is not available." He then summarized this
work by commenting that "the Identi-kit seems to be a pretty lousy
procedure for generating faces." In another more recent study he
is engaged in, subjects were *initially* shown a sketch or composite
and then the target. Results from this study indicate that sketches
lead to clearly better recognition responses over composites.

Goldstein's (1977) excellent review of psychological literature
which bears on eyewitness testimony, along with his thoughtful
analysis and recommendations, are well worth scrutinizing. As he
points out, there is a dramatic difference between the ability of a
person to recognize a face given *multiple exposures* versus the
ability to recognize a face given a brief *single exposure*. Yet
lawyers and jurists apparently do not draw this distinction. The
aforementioned cross-sectional study of high school graduates

(Bahrick, Bahrick, and Wittlinger, 1975) helps to support his contention that repeated exposures to a face greatly assist in the recognition process. Another interesting point, consistent with the literature reviewed, is that in some of the experiments subjects *knew* they would be asked to make a later identification. They thus had an advantage not afforded by real-life cases in which witnesses in criminal cases are later asked to make identifications.

Comparisons between photographs and live models and photographs and videotape yield interesting results. In a comparison of live models vs. photographs, Adkins, Egan, Peterson, Pittner, and Goldstein (1974) found that recognition of live models was not superior to recognition of photographs. Also, and of critical importance to the criminal justice system, *misidentifications* occurred frequently. Forty-four percent of the subjects who accurately identified one target erroneously selected a decoy as a second target. In a research study designed to compare monochromatic (black and white) video sequences with monochromatic (black and white) still photography and color still photography, Sussman, Sugarman and Zavala (1972) found that both videotape and color still photography were superior to the black and white still photography in a recognition task. The authors commented: "The implication is that even though the video was in black and white, the dynamic cues offered by video improved identification as much over black and white still photography as does color still photography. In other words, about an equal improvement in identification was obtained by use of color as by use of dynamic imagery. This result is important because it suggests strongly that color video may well yield additional improvement over still photography or over black and white video" (p. 311). Law enforcement personnel tend to believe, perhaps correctly, that corporeal (live) identifications are superior to photographs as far as ease of recognition is concerned.

Goldstein's (1977) analysis lead him to suggest a radical departure in the way eyewitness testimony is treated:

> Because of the fundamental inherent nature of eyewitness unreliability, I propose that eyewitness identification testimony no longer be admissible as evidence when it is *the only class of evidence* available in a criminal trial. I would even go further and propose that no

official police action should be taken on the basis of eyewitness testimony alone; to be formally accused of a crime is quite serious—tantamount to guilt, according to some lawyers—and could be inordinately expensive in terms of money, time, and personal anguish even though no trial ever ensues. Furthermore, eyewitness personal identification testimony should be inadmissible unless corroborated by facts associated with another class of evidence. (p. 237)

I shall return to Goldstein's suggested reform at a later point in the next chapter when I set forth my own views.

EYEWITNESS TESTIMONY AND PSYCHOLOGICAL EXPERIMENTATION

In this section, a number of studies that employ simulations of actual criminal eyewitness reports are presented. While studies of this type are sometimes less susceptible to the tight experimental controls prized by some behavioral scientists, due to the fact that they embrace so many variables, they enjoy the advantage of resembling the actual situation that eyewitnesses are called upon to cope with in criminal cases. The previously discussed problems associated with perception and memory are combined with the added difficulties of what Marshall (1963) called "Articulation" or reporting.

Nonverbal Cues and Photographic Identification

Mehrabian (1970), in his work on nonverbal behavior, suggests that hand movement, body posture, facial expression, eye contact, and tone of voice are more reflective of a person's attitudes than his verbal statements. Many psychotherapists would concur with his findings, although they often view nonverbal cues as indicative of unconscious processes.

Fanselow and Buckhout (1976) presented a film of a criminal assault to psychology student subjects. In the film the face of the black assailant was clearly visible for four seconds. Similar to the photographic arrays used by police, a researcher presented six color photographs of black men whose age, height, weight, build, and skin tone matched those of the attacker presented on the film. Three experimental procedures were used. In the first instance *(positive condition),* a randomly selected group of subjects were exposed to the photographs, and the person who administered the photo array provided the nonverbal cues of smiling, leaning forward and eye contact to cue the "witnesses." In the *neutral condition,* the treatment was "erect body posture, looking at the subject's kneecap and blank facial expression." For the third condition, which the researchers termed *negative,* the presenter looked away from the subject, leaned backward, frowned and fidgeted. For the groups exposed to the *positive* or *negative* condition only the target person received the special cueing effects. The "offender's" photo was not shown in the arrays presented to subjects, only innocent parties.

Results demonstrated that both the *negative* and *positive* conditions were equally successful in eliciting erroneous identifications from suspects. In the *negative* condition, 16 percent picked the cued target; in the *positive* conditions, 22.8 percent of the subjects selected the target designated by the presenter (however, differences between groups were statistically nonsignificant). *What is more impressive is that most of the subjects attempted identifications, notwithstanding the fact that the "suspect's photo (the person shown in the filmed criminal assault) was not included.* An average of 72 percent picked photos other than the one cued by presenters. Thus, only 13 percent (average) declined to select someone. In a second related experiment in which the photo of the attacker was shown along with five decoys, only 25 percent of the subjects correctly identified the assailant while 90 percent attempted an identification (Buckhout and Ellison, 1977).

Another experiment conducted by Buckhout et al. (Buckhout, Figueroa, and Hoff, 1975), involved a manipulation of a photo in arrays presented in two groups. Both groups observed a staged crime in a classroom and they were asked if they could recognize the perpetrator. The group exposed to the biased condition viewed a photo array in which one photograph was tilted and the facial expression was changed from a smile to a scowl. The biased photo was picked more than others although it was actually an "innocent party." Additional information that resulted from this study included the fact that witnesses overestimated the weight of the suspect by 25 pounds while they closely estimated his actual height. The time span of the incident was overestimated by two and one half to one. Almost as an aside, Buckhout et al. state that they have administered the biased photo spread to groups of "non-witnesses" who were given only a general description of the crime, with the result that even these parties picked the unusual photo more often than others.

The use of photos by police to assist them in criminal investigations is relatively common. While it appears to be an important instrument in criminal investigations of suspects, it is not without its problems as Wall (1965) pointed out:

> In considering the effect which the use of photographs may have upon the reliability of an identification, there are a number of principles which must be recognized, and the first is that where a photograph has been identified as that of the guilty party, any subsequent corporeal identification of that person may be based not upon the witness's recollection of the features of the guilty party, but upon his recollection of the photograph. Thus, although a witness who is asked to attempt a corporeal identification of a person whose photograph he has previously identified may say, "That's the man that did it," what he may actually mean is, "That's the man whose photograph I identified." (p. 68)

Another factor that Wall (1965) raises concerning the unreliability of photographic identifications has to do with the quality of the photo iteslf. He points out that it is two-dimensional rather than three and it presents a "frozen" image which may be quite different from the living objects which it represents. Furthermore, a police photograph may be old and at variance with the subject who himself has aged and/or who may have chosen to change his appearance. For these reasons, among others, Wall (1965) suggests that photographic identifications are inferior to corporeal identifications and should be used only when other alternatives are lacking. A recent comment offered by a member of the Manhattan District Attorney's office is consistent with this approach. He states that lineups are clearly preferred over photographic identifications. As the reader may recall, in the case of Oscar Slater a number of witnesses had identified him from a photo prior to a lineup identification. Surely, this did nothing to minimize the overall prejudice and bias that characterized this case.

Research recently completed on this subject (Egan, Pittner and Goldstein, 1979), confirms Wall's (1965) earlier contentions concerning photo vs. corporeal identification.   In a laboratory study approach three groups of eyewitnesses viewed two target persons through a one-way window and were tested for accuracy of identification following periods of two, twenty-one, or fifty-six days. Subjects were asked to make either "live" or photographic identifications. In both presentation methods, only one of the original two targets was offered in the five-person arrays. *Five targets were more accurately identified than photographs of targets (97% vs. 85%) and this difference was true for female as well as male subjects and at all delay intervals.* Also, deterioration in identification performance was generally found to increase over time.

In conclusion, the authors stressed the importance of the findings associated with "hit" rates as "false alarms."   The investigators noted that while the hit rate, the accurate selecting of the target in the test situation (photo array or mock lineup), was near perfect, the number of individuals who erroneously selected a second individual was also high.   Specifically, 67 percent of the subjects selected two men, one of whom was erroneously chosen. Only 28 percent of the subjects did not commit an error.

In the area of eyewitness identification research, it is understandable that attention would be directed at both laboratory and field research which concentrates on facial identity.   However, other behavioral characteristics of the suspect probably play a role in an identification at a lineup.   The way a person walks, for example, may be revealing. If not sufficient in itself, it may be an additional cue relied upon by the witness. Some administrators of lineups do require the participants to walk around, although frequently they are asked to walk just a few paces. The work of Cutting and Kozlowski (1977) represents an interesting thrust into this area of behavioral research. Viewers were able to recognize themselves and others in an abstract display of their movements. Light sources were mounted on joints prominent during the act of walking and were sufficient cues for identification.

Experimental Analogues of Eyewitness Accounts

One way to test the fairness of a lineup is to discover if uninvolved people with practically no knowledge of the suspect can pick him out beyond chance or, in other words, is he chosen statistically more often than others? This is the view offered by Doob and Kirshenbaum (1973) in their article on police lineups. The authors discuss the frequently-referred-to problems of dissimilar appearing individuals in a lineup, expectations aroused by asking a witness to come in and view a lineup, and the problem posed by a witness who rehearses the description given to police prior to viewing a lineup.

Specifically, they report on the case of *R v. Shatford*. In this case, a witness offered the statement that, "they were very neatly dressed, and rather good looking and they looked enough alike to be brothers." Several days after giving the above-mentioned description of the bank robbers, she participated with other witnesses in the drawing of a "composite picture" of the suspect, although she admitted she really was unable to offer anything distinctive concerning their features. The lineup which eventually took place was not a good one, according to the authors, because five of the eleven decoys wore glasses while the accused did not; the accused did not wear a tie, yet eleven of the other lineup participants wore ties; six of the decoys could be described as round-faced or beefy, whereas the suspect had been described as having "high cheek bones and a v-shaped face." The witness picked out the suspect, and according to Doob and Kirshenbaum (1973), the "good looking" description may have actually been the key. While acknowledging its general subjective quality, a group of twenty female students was asked to rate the attractiveness of the lineup participants from a photograph of the twelve men. The suspect was picked more frequently than the others.

If these subjects had been asked to pick out a criminal suspect, they might nonetheless have picked out a different party if a second experiment was run. Because of this possibility, twenty-one new subjects were shown the lineup photograph and eleven chose the suspect. This is well above a chance occurrence, of course, and suggests that with this particular lineup the phrase "he was rather good looking" was a critical cue.

In a study of the possible effects of dogmatism (closed mindedness) on eyewitness testimony, Hatton and Snortum (1971) arranged an experimental situation in which three groups viewed a film of a pedestrian and automobile accident. In the *first* group, thirty subjects were informed that "the driver had a record of four recent traffic citations and was once arrested for assault." The woman was presented as a mother who had completed a tour of duty as a volunteer at a nearby children's hospital. In the *second* condition, a different group of thirty subjects were told that eighteen months prior to this incident, the woman had sued for a whiplash injury, but it had later been dropped because of "failure to find medical substantiation for her claim." The man was described as a father who was just returning from some extra office work where he was employed as a social worker who assisted mental retardates. The *third* group (control) received no biasing information.

In this study, subjects generally registered stronger agreement with antivictim statements than with antidriver statements. The authors speculate whether this reflects male chauvinism (in response to the male driver and female victim) or whether the antivictim statements were more influential in their impact. Not unexpectedly, higher ratings of confidence were assigned to the neutral fact items answered correctly than those answered incorrectly. There was no evidence that dogmatic subjects placed more confidence in their answers nor was there any support for the hypothesis that dogmatic subjects would be more likely to reconstruct events of the accident in a pattern to fit the biasing information. Inconsistent with the general findings on perception and eyewitness testimony, Hatton and Snortum (1971) state in their conclusion that the results "generally support the notion that if there is strict adherence to judicial procedures which limit witness testimony to direct observations, the effects of observer bias may be held within tolerable limits." This statement is in such marked contrast with the scholarly literature in this field that it must be seriously questioned. Among other issues, the authors' methodology, which included the use of paper and pencil questionnaire devices, raises questions concerning the validity of their findings. Equally important, the authors appear to have gone well beyond their data in expressing such a broad generalization in their concluding statement.

In one of the largest studies of eyewitness testimony ever conducted, Buckhout (1975) employed a previously used film (staged) of a mugging and arranged for it to be presented on New York's Channel 4 (NBC-TV). The film allowed for a direct facial view of the offender. Immediately afterward, the announcer presented a lineup of six men who approximated the description of the assailant. T.V. viewers were instructed that the criminal suspect might or might not be in the lineup. In response to a large number of phone calls received (over 2145 before the calls were cut off), Buckhout reports the following findings:

1. Only 14 percent of the viewers correctly identified the assailant.
2. There were no differences (statistically) between any of the choices of lineup participants selected, which would be no different if viewers were merely guessing.
3. Males and females did not differ as witnesses.

The author is quick to point out the limitations of this large-scale attempt to study eyewitness observations:

1. The televised picture may not have been of high quality.
2. The witnesses may have been viewing in color or black and white or on different-sized screens.
3. The nature of sampling errors was unknown.

Offered somewhat as an aside, Buckhout (1975) notes that in subsequent showings of the film to smaller groups, "In New York, many of our witnesses (34%) described the attacker as Hispanic or Puerto Rican. When the film was shown in Washington, D.C., those witnesses who mislabeled the race of the attacker called him black. In fact, the perpetrator in the film was a Jewish man with a somewhat dark complexion. We had, surprisingly, found that the uncertainty of some witnesses leads them to attribute a stereotyped norm for criminals—New Yorkers see Hispanic, while Washingtonians see black" (p. 4).

The value of an object may bear some relationship to the witness' ability to make an identification (Leippe, Wells, and Ostrom, 1978). Experimentally, these researchers demonstrated that when male and female subjects viewed a staged theft, and when the witnesses had prior knowledge of the object's value, accurate identification of the suspect was more likely when the theft was of high rather than low seriousness. Seriousness (high or low) did not affect identification when the knowldege was gained after the "crime." Also, certainty of choice in the identification task was unrelated to accuracy of choice.

Type of Questioning/Interrogation and Its Effect on Accuracy of Eyewitness Reports

A number of scholars have been interested in the way in which the questioning of witnesses may affect their testimony. The earliest work on this subject (Stern, 1939; Whipple, 1909; Cady, 1924; Whitely and McGeoch, 1927) was reviewed briefly in the introductory chapter of this volume. Briefly, the early work noted that notwithstanding witnesses' good intentions, they rarely provided completely accurate reports and errors tended to increase when specific questions were asked as opposed to more spontaneous narrative testimony.

The first research investigation to be considered in this area is one in which the authors (Clifford and Scott, 1978) studied the mode of questioning, yet were primarily concerned about the emotionality or arousal effects of certain types of crime (violent or nonviolent). Concerning the emotional impact of a crime on a witness, this study is thus linked to the one reported on above (Leippe, Wells, and Ostrom, 1978). Groups of male and female undergraduates were assigned to a variety of conditions. Some subjects viewed a nonviolent videotape while others witnessed a similar tape which substituted a brief violent incident for a nonviolent one.

A main finding of the study was the significantly poorer recall of witnesses who observed the violent as compared with nonviolent taped segment. Recall of both physical actions and physical descriptions was less accurate in the violent film. While no differences existed between the sexes in their reports on the nonviolent incident, women were less accurate in the violent condition. A study reported on later by Lipton (1977) is contradictory—women provided more accurate reports to a violent scene.

Concerning recall accuracy in narrative vs. interrogative reporting, no differences were found. As noted earlier, research by Cady (1924) and Marston (1924) found differences on the type of questioning but outcome from other studies discussed in this section are more consistent with those of the present authors. Leading questions played a critical role with only 5 percent of the subjects avoiding being misled by at least one question. Personality differences, as measured by a scale of introversion-extraversion, did not correlate with accuracy of report. One final item that appears to have important implications for the criminal justice field is that "certainty of correctness" was not significantly related to "objective accuracy."

Marquis, Marshall and Oskamp (1972) studied the validity of testimony as a function of the question form, atmosphere, and item difficulty. A short (1 minute, 55 seconds) film, depicting an auto striking a woman, was shown to 151 adult male subjects. Researchers identified 884 scorable facts in the film.

Regarding the atmosphere provided in postfilm interviews, the researchers found that witnesses who were *challenged* (as compared to the *supportive* condition) tended to like the interviewer less as a person, demonstrated less liking for the manner in which he conducted the questioning, and believed the interviewer thought poorly of their performance. More importantly, though, the atmosphere had no important effect on accuracy or completeness of testimony.

As question specificity increased, there was an increase in the amount of material covered in testimony and a decrease in the overall accuracy of testimony. Accuracy was highest for free reports, next highest for the two open-ended interviews, and slightly lower for the interrogations using specific questions and force-choice answers.

Concerning item difficulty, accuracy was high for both easy and difficult items. For structured questions, accuracy was high for easy items, but very low for difficult items. As the authors (Marquis, Marshall & Oskamp, 1972) note, "The trade-off between accuracy and completeness was mediated by item difficulty. It was pronounced for items of high difficulty and not apparent for items of low difficulty" (p. 167).

In one of the classic experiments on eyewitness testimony, Marshall (1966) compared the perceptions of 167 law students with 102 police trainees, and twenty-two settlement house residents. The subjects were shown a short (42 seconds) film in which a boy approached a baby carriage, observed what appeared to be an infant for a few moments, and then started to move the carriage before being startled by a woman shouting at him. The film then showed him running through the gate of the yard and attempting to hide by a white picket fence. Researchers identified 115 possible items in the film. Subjects were given questionnaires immediately after the film showing and one week later Marshall (1966) summarized his findings as follows:

> Where there is a greater verbal capacity, there is greater correct recall and there are a greater number of inferences but a lower ratio of inferences to correct recall. Within each socioeducational group, where there is high punitiveness, there is greater recall and less where there is low punitiveness. When a status figure urges subjects to do well there is a greater number of inferences by law students and less by the police trainees than by their control group. Among the law students, those who were told that they would be witnesses for the prosecution had greater recall than those who were told that they would be witnesses for the defendants. (p. 81)

The way in which a question is phrased can exert a powerful influence on what a witness remembers (Loftus, 1974). In an initial study, Loftus (1974) and her assistants arranged an experiment in which 100 students viewed a short film segment depicting a multiple-car accident. Immediately afterward the subjects were asked to complete short questionnaires which contained six critical items. Three questions referred to items that had appeared in the film whereas three inquired about items not present in the film.

For half the subjects, the key questions began with the phrase, "Did you see a _____?" as in "Did you see a broken headlight?" The other subjects received questions which were phrased, "Did you see the _____?" as in "Did you see the broken headlight?" The form of the article, *the* or *a,* was the only distinguishing feature of the questions. The results demonstrated that this minor change, what is commonly referred to as a *leading question,* had a significant impact. Witnesses who were asked *the* question were more likely to report having seen something, whether or not it had really appeared in the film, than those who were asked *a* questions.

In a second study, subjects were asked to estimate the speed of a vehicle involved in an accident presented on film (Loftus, 1974). The verb used in the question asked of witnesses—*smashed, collided, bumped,* or *contacted*—influenced the estimated speed reported by subjects. Generally, the findings indicated that people were not very good at judging the actual speed. *Smashed* consistently elicited higher estimates than *collided, bumped,* or *contacted.*

In a demonstration of the excessive weight afforded an eyewitness report, Loftus (1974) simulated a jury trial in which 150 students acted as jurors. After receiving a written description of a store robbery and a summary of the evidence, the subjects were divided into several groups. One group was told that there had been no eyewitnesses; another was told that a store clerk testified that he saw the defendant shoot the two victims, although the defense attorney claimed he was mistaken. Finally, a third group of students were told that the store clerk had testified to seeing the shooting, but the defense attorney had discredited him. The attorney claimed that the man, whose vision was poorer than 20/40, had not been wearing his glasses and could not possibly have seen the face of the robber from his position.

Notwithstanding the discrediting of the witness, 68 percent of those subjects voted guilty, while 72 percent of those who had been told there was a witness (who the defense attorney stated was mistaken), voted guilty. Only 18 percent of those who were informed there was no eyewitness voted for a guilty verdict.

In a later series of experiments (Loftus, 1975), a total of 490 college student subjects saw films of fast moving events—automobile accidents or classroom disruptions. The investigator was interested in determining if the questions asked immediately after an event might affect responses to questions much later. Results indicated that when the initial question contained either true presuppositions (postulated the existence of an object that did exist in the scene) or false presuppositions (postulated the existence of an object that did *not* exist), the likelihood was increased that subjects would later report having seen the presupposed object. Loftus (1975) suggests that "questions asked immediately after an event can introduce new—not necessarily correct—information, which is then added to the memorial representation of the event, thereby causing its reconstruction or alteration" (p. 560) .

Williams (1975) was interested in examining responses to written vs. oral forms of interrogation. In the same study, she also explored the problem posed by the witness who later responds to the original description given by the perpetrator rather than the actual person who appeared in a lineup. This second problem was investigated through the use of a "personal description probe," identical to one employed by the New York City Police Department. This broad description probe uses a checklist of every possible personal characteristic of any suspect, fragmenting the original perception into parts. Subjects were 121 Brooklyn College undergraduate students registered in an introductory psychology course. The stimulus event was a nine-second film which depicted a mugging and shooting of one male by another.

The researcher (Williams, 1975) found that the *verbal* mode of interrogation produced far more accurate recall data from witnesses than the *written* mode. Related to this finding, however, was the fact that the number of correct identifications was not different for *verbal* vs. *written* interrogation modes. Subjects had been asked to see if they could recognize the "perpetrator" from a photo spread (lineup) . Williams (1975) suggested that the reason for the latter finding seemed to be due to the fact that witnesses generally did poorly at recognizing the offender. Results from the second variable studied, the effect of the personal description probe upon subsequent ability to make an identification, indicated that rather than aiding the witnesses' memories, it merely encouraged them to "try harder" (attempt more recognitions) at the expense of accuracy.

Concerning the better response of subjects to the *verbal* interrogation, the author correctly points out that the actual experience of witnesses who are verbally interrogated may be far different. The police station house represents a more threatening atmosphere and of course the witness may fear retaliation at the hands of the suspect. Over one-third of the witnesses were mistaken about the suspect's race. As was noted previously in this chapter, stereotypes are commonplace and prejudiced feelings frequently add elements to the identification process.

The Buckout group at Brooklyn College (Alper, Buckhout, Chern, Harwood and Slomovits, 1976) became interested in comparing group recollections of a criminal act with individual recollections. They viewed a staged incident of a crime in a classroom atmosphere. Subjects were twenty-nine undergraduate students at Brooklyn College enrolled in a course in social psychology. The work of Asch and his colleagues on group conformity and group pressure provided a stimulus for the study.

Similar to findings reported on earlier by Clifford and Scott (1968), these researchers found a large disparity between the confidence with which individuals as well as groups reported their observations and the actual data they provided. Initially, individual eyewitness reports were gathered and then individuals were placed in groups to discuss their recollections and reach a consensus on their observations. The main finding was that while group decisions resulted in more *complete* information, this completeness was at the expense of larger numbers of errors of commission, what the authors refer to as "the fabrication of details under group pressure." The pooled descriptions were superior to what any of the individual "witnesses" reported. Finally, in commenting on their results, the authors note that while the more *complete* descriptions offered by pooling witness information have a certain appeal to criminal investigators, the inaccuracies attendant to such a process make this approach less desirable. More importantly, however, the U.S. Supreme Court in *Wade* and in other opinions has discussed the importance of an *independent* source in a witness' identification.

The final study to be reported on in this cluster of investigations that have focused on relationships between the type of reporting, questioning and accuracy of recall is one undertaken by Lipton (1977). It was a master's thesis written at California State University at Northridge. Lipton found that a delay between a witness' observations and later testimony "adversely affects the accuracy and quantity" of information. Question phrasing did have a significant impact on the testimony provided: unstructured testimony tended to be very accurate but incomplete, while structured testimony was more complete but less accurate. Furthermore, leading questions did shape the testimony provided by witnesses. Finally, female witnesses gave more accurate testimony than males.

CONCLUSION

A great variety of psychological issues have been discussed that are germane to eyewitness testimony. The following chapter summarizes and provides analysis of some of the more important legal issues in this area. At the end of that chapter, the author presents an overall outline of the critical issues that need to be considered in judging the validity of eyewitness accounts.

REFERENCES

Adams, J.A. Human Memory. New York: McGraw-Hill, 1967.

Adkins, C., Egan, D., Peterson, L., Pittner, M., and Goldstein, A. The Effects of Exposure Delay, and Method of Presentation of Eye-Witness Identification. Unpublished manuscript, 1974.

Allport, G.W. and Postman, L.F. The Basic Psychology of Rumor. In E.F. Maccoby, T.M. Newcomb, and E.L. Hartley (Eds.) *Readings in Social Psychology*. New York: Holt, Rinehart & Winston, 1958.

Alper, A., Buckhout, R., Chen, S., Harwood, R., and Slomovits, M. Eyewitness Identification: Accuracy of Individual vs. Composite Recollections of a Crime. *Bulletin of the Psychonomic Society*, 1976, 8, 147-149.

Asch, S. Opinions and Social Pressure. *Scientific American*, 1955, 193, 31-35.

Bahrick, H., Bahrick, P., and Wittlinger, R. Fifty Years of Memory for Names and Faces: A Cross-Sectional Approach. *Journal of Experimental Psychology: General*, 1975, 104, 54-75.

Bower, G. and Karlin, M. Depth of Processing Pictures of Faces and Recognition Memory. *Journal of Experimental Psychology*, 1974, 103, 751-757.

Borchard, E.M. *Convicting the Innocent*. New Haven: Yale University Press, 1932.

Brody, R. Mugged Once, But Victimized Twice. *New York Times*, May 16, 1978, Op-Ed Page.

Brooks, R., and Goldstein, A. Recognition of Children of Inverted Photographs of Faces. *Child Development*, 1963, 34, 1033-1040.

Bruner, J.S. On Perceptual Readiness. *Psychological Review*, 1957, 64, 123-152.

Bruner, J.S. Social Psychology and Perception. In E.F. Maccoby, T.M. Newcomb, and E.L. Hartley, (Eds.) *Readings in Social Psychology*. New York: Holt, Rinehart & Winston, 1958.

Bruner, J.S. *Beyond the Information Given*. New York: W.W. Norton Co., 1973.

Bruner, J.S. and Goodman, C.C. Value and Need as Organizing Factors in Perception. *Journal of Abnormal and Social Psychology*, 1947, 42, 33-44.

Bruner, J.S. and Postman, L. Emotional Selectivity in Perception and Reaction. *Journal of Personality*, 1947, 16, 69-77.

Burner, J.S. and Potter, M.C. Interference in Visual Recognition. *Science*, 44, 424-425.

Buckhout, R. Need for Social Approval and Dyadic Verbal Behavior. *Psychological Reports*, 1965, 16, 1013-1016.

Buckhout, R. Eyewitness Testimony. *Scientific American*, 1974, 212, 23-31.

Buckhout, R. Nearly 2000 Witnesses Can Be Wrong. *Report No. CR-22*, 1975, Center for Responsive Psychology, Brooklyn College, City University of New York.

Buckhout, R. Psychology and Eyewitness Identification. *Report No. CR-1*, Center for Responsive Psychology, Brooklyn College, 1975.

Buckhout, R., Alper, A., Chern, S., Silverberg, G. and Slomovits, M. Determinants of Eyewitness Performance On a Lineup. *Bulletin of the Psychonomic Society*, 1974, 191-192.

Buckhout, R. and Ellison, K. The Line-Up: A Critical Look. *Psychology Today*, June, 1977, 81-84.

Buckhout, R., Figueroa, D. and Hoff, E. Eyewitness Identification: Effects of Suggestion and Bias in Identification From Photographs. *Bulletin of the Psychonomic Society*, 1975, 71-74.

Cady, H. On the Psychology of Testimony. *American Journal of Psycology*, 1924, 35, 110-112.

Chance, J., Goldstein, A. and McBride, L. Differential Experience and Recognition Memory For Faces. *The Journal of Social Psychology*, 1975, 97, 243-253.

Cutting, J. and Kozlowski, L. Recognizing Friends By Their Walk: Gait Perception Without Familiarity Cues. *Bulletin of the Psychonomic Society*, 1977, 9, 353-356.

Davies, G., Ellis, H., and Shepherd, J. Face Recognition Accuracy As a Function of Mode of Representation. *Journal of Applied Psychology*, 1978, 63, 180-187.

Davies, G., Shepherd, J., and Ellis, M. Effects of Interpolated Mugshot Exposure on Accuracy of Eyewitness Identification. *Journal of Applied Psychology*, 1979, 64, 232-237.

Doob, A. and Kirschenbaum, H. Bias in Police Lineups—Partial Remembering. *Journal of Police Science and Administration*, 1973, 1, 287-293.

Edmonton Journal. Cleared Priest "Knew All Along" He Was Free Man, August 24, 1979, A13.

Egan, D., Pittner, M. and Goldstein, A. Eyewitness Identification, Photographs vs. Live Models. *Human Behavior and Law*, Spring, 1979.

Erdelyi, M.H. A New Look at the New Look: Perceptual Defense and

Vigilance. *Psychological Review,* 1974, 81, 1-25.

Fanselow, M. and Buckhout, R. Non-Verbal Cueing as a Source of Biasing Information In Eyewitness Identification Testing. Report No. CR-26, Center for Responsive Psychology, Brooklyn College, 1976.

Forbes, D. An Investigation Into Pictorial Memory With Particular Reference to Facial Recognition. Unpublished Doctoral Dissertation, Aberdeen University, 1975.

Gerard, R.W. What Is Memory. *Scientific American,* 1953, 210, 118-126.

Gilbert v. California 388 U.S. 263, *Supreme Court Reporter,* 1967.

Goldstein, A.V. The Fallibility of the Eyewitness: Psychological Evidence. In B.D. Sales (Ed.), *Psychology In the Legal Process.* New York: Spectrum Publications, Inc., 1977.

Goldstein, A., and Chance, J. Recognition of Children's Face. *Child Development,* 1964, 35, 129-136.

Goldstein, A. and Chance, J. Visual Recognition Memory for Complex Configurations. *Perception and Psychophysics,* 1970, 9, 237-241.

Goldstein, A., and Chance, J. Intraindividual Consistency in Visual Recognition Memory. Paper presented at American Psychological Association Convention, August 31, 1978, Toronto, Canada.

Goldstein, A., Stephenson, B. and Chance, J. Face Recognition Memory: Distribution of False Alarms. *Bulletin of the Psychonomic Society,* 1977, 9, 416-418.

Hatton, D. and Snortum, J. The Effects of Biasing Information and Dogmatism Upon Witness Testimony. *Psychonomic Science,* 1971, 23, 425-427.

Hilgard, E.R., Atkinson, R.C., and Atkinson, R.L. *Introduction To Psychology.* New York: Harcourt, Brace, Jovanovich, Inc., 1975.

James, L. Differential Face Recognition and Stereotyped Perception. Unpublished doctoral dissertation from Ohio State University, 1976.

Jones, E.E. and deCharms, R. Changes in Social Perception As a Function of the Personal Relevance of Behavior. In E.F. Maccoby and T.M. Newcomb (Eds.) *Readings in Social Psycholgy.* New York: Holt, Rinehart and Winston, 1958.

Kirby v. Illinois 406 U.S. 682. *Supreme Court Reporter,* 1971.

Lane, A. Effects of Pose Position on Identification. In A. Zavala and J. Paley, *Personal Appearance Identification.* Springfield, Illinois: Charles C Thomas, Publisher, 1972.

Laughery, K., Alexander, J. and Lane, A. Recognition of Human Faces: Effect of Target Exposure Time, Target Position, Pose Position, and Type of Photograph. *Journal of Applied Psychology,* 1971, 55, 477-483.

Laughery, K., Fessler, P., Lenorovitz, D., and Yoblick, D. Time Delay and Similarity Effects in Facial Recognition. *Journal of Applied Psychology,* 1974, 59, 490-496.

Laughery, K., and Fowler, R. Analysis of Procedures for Generating Facial Images. American Psychological Convention, August 31, 1978, Toronto, Canada.

Leippe, M., Wells, G. and Ostrom, T. Crime Seriousness As a Determinant of Accuracy in Eyewitness Identification. *Journal of Applied Psychology,* 1978, 63, 345-351.

Levine, R., Chein, I. and Murphy, G. The Relationship of the Intensity of Need to the Amount of Perceptual Distortion: A Preliminary Report. *Journal of Psychology,* 1942, 13, 283-293.

Levine, J.M. and Murphy, G. The Learning and Forgetting of Controversial Material. *Journal of Abnormal and Social Psychology,* 1943, 38, 507-517.

Levine, F.J. and Tapp, J.L. The Psychology of Criminal Identification: The Gap from Wade to Kirby. *University of Pennsylvania Law Review,* 1973, 121, 1079-1131.

Lipton, J. On the Psychology of Eyewitness Testimony. *Journal of Applied Psychology,* 1977, 62, 90-95.

Loftus, E. Reconstructing Memory, the Incredible Eyewitness. *Psychology Today,* 1974, December, 117-119.

Loftus, E. Leading Questions and the Eyewitness Report. *Cognitive Psycology,* 1975, 7, 650-672.

Malpass, R.S. and Kravitz, J. Recognition for Faces of Own and Other "Race." *Journal of Personality and Social Psychology,* 1969, 13, 330-335.

Marquis, K., Marshall, J. and Oskamp, S. Testimony Validity as a Function of Question Form, Atmosphere, and Item Difficulty. *Journal of Applied Social Psychology,* 1972, 2, 167-186.

Marshall, J. Evidence, Psychology, and the Trial: Some Challenges to Law. *Columbia Law Review,* 1963, 63, 197-231.

Marshall, J. *Law and Psychology in Conflict.* Indianapolis: The Bobbs-Merrill Company, Inc., 1966.

McG. Thomas, Jr., R. Reluctance of Witnesses Hampers Inquiries in Two Brooklyn Slayings, *New York Times,* October 25, 1977.

McGinnies, E. Emotional and Perceptual Defense. *Psychological Review,* 1949, 56, 244-251.

Mehrabian, A. *Tactics of Social Influence.* New Jersey: Prentice, Hall, Inc., 1970.

Miller, G.R. and Boster, F.J. Effects of Type of Evidence on Judgments of Likelihood of Conviction and Certainty of Guilt. Unpublished Manuscript, Department of Communication, Michigan State University, 1975. Reported in B.D. Sales (Ed.), *Psychology in the Legal Process,* New York: Spectrum Publications, Inc., 1977.

Moore v. Illinois 46 *U.S.L.W.,* December 13, 1977.

Morgan, C.T. *Perception: A Brief Introduction to Psychology.* New York: McGraw-Hill, 1974.

Mueller, J. Levels of Processing and Facial Recognition. Paper presented at the American Psychological Association Convention, August 31, 1978, Toronto, Canada.

Murdock, B.B. Memory. In P. Mussen and R. R. Rosenzweig: *Psychology An Introduction.* Lexington, Massachusetts: D. C. Health and Company, 1973.

Neil v. Biggers 409 U.S. 188. *Supreme Court Reporter,* 1972.

New York Post. F.B.I. Joins Bombing Probes, May 15, 1978.

Orne, M. On the Social Psychology of the Psychological Experiment: With Particular Reference to Demand Characteristics and Their Implications. Paper presented at the American Psychological Convention, New York, 1961.

Penfield, W. Memory Mechanisms. A.M. *Archives of Neurology and Psychiatry,* 1952, 67, 178-198.

Pettigrew, T.F., Allport, G.W. and Barnett, E.O. Binocular Resolution and Perception of Race in South Africa. *British Journal of Psychology,* 1958.

Raab, S. Robbery Conviction Poses Question on Evidence. *New York Times,* January 31, 1978, 29.

Rokeach, M. *The Open and Closed Mind.* New York: Basic Books, Inc., 1960.

Rolph, C.H. *Personal Identity.* London: Michael Joseph, 1957.

Rosenthal, R. *Experimenter Effects in Behavioral Research.* New York: Appleton-Century-Crofts, 1966.

Scodel, A. and Austrin, H. The Perception of Jewish Photographs by Non-Jews and Jews, *Journal of Abnormal Social Psychology,* 1957, 54, 278-280.

Secord, P.F., Bevan W. and Dukes, W.G. Occupational and Physiognomic Stereotypes in the Perception of Photographs. *The Journal of Social Psychology,* 1953, 37, 261-270.

Secord, P.F., Bevan, W. and Katz, B. The Negro Stereotype and Perceptual Accentuation. *Journal of Abnormal Social Psychology,* 1956, 53, 78-83.

Shepherd, J.W. and Ellis, H.D. The Effect of Attractiveness on Recognition Memory for Faces. *American Journal of Psychology,* 1973, 86, 627-633.

Shoemaker, D.J., South, D.R. and Lowe, J. Facial Stereotypes of Deviants and Judgments of Guilt or Innocence. *Social Forces,* 1973, 51, 427-433.

Shrauger, S., and Altrocchi, J. The Personality of the Perceiver as a Factor in Person Perception. *Psychological Bulletin,* 62, 297-298.

Siegel, S. Certain Determinants and Correlates of Authoritarianism. *Genetic Psychological Monograph,* 1954, 49, 187-229.

Sobel, N. *Eye-Witness Identification: Legal and Practical Problems.* New York: Clark Boardman Company, Ltd., 1972.

Sobel, N. *Supplement to Eye-Witness Identification: Legal and Practical Problems.* New York: Clark Boardman Company, Ltd., 1978.

Stern, L.W. The Psychology of Testimony. *Journal of Abnormal and*

Social Psychology, 1939, 32, 3-20.

Stovall v. Denno 388 U.S. 293. *Supreme Court Reporter,* 1967.

Struad, B. and Mueller, J.   Levels of Processing in Facial Recognition Memory. *Bulletin of the Psychonomic Society,* 1977, 9, 17-18.

Sussman, E., Sugarman, R. and Zavala, A.   A Comparison of Three Media Used in Identification Procedures. In a Zavala and J. Paley *Personal Appearance Identification.* Springfield, Illinois: Charles C Thomas, Publisher, 1972.

United States v. Wade 388 U.S. 218. *Supreme Court Reporter,* 1967.

Uviller, R.   *The Processes of Criminal Justice: Investigation and Adjudication* (supplement). St. Paul, Minnesota: West, 1977.

Wall, P.   *Eye-Witness Identification in Criminal Cases.*   Springfield, Illinois: Charles C Thomas, Publisher, 1965.

Wertheimer, M.   The Creativity of Perception.   In P. Mussen and M.R. Rosenzweig (Ed.)   *Psychology An Introduction.*   Lexington, Massachusetts: D. C. Heath and Company, 1973.

Whipple, G.   The Observer As Reporter. *Psychological Bulletin,* 1909, 6, 153-170.

Whitely, P. and McGeoch, J.   The Effect of One Form of Report Upon Another. *American Journal of Psychology,* 1927, 38, 280-284.

Williams, L.   Application of Signal Detection Parameters in a Test of Eyewitnesses To a Crime.   Report No. CR-20, 1975.   Center for Responsive Psychology, Brooklyn College, City University of New York.

Yarmey, D.   Recognition Memory for Male and Female Faces.   Paper presented at American Psychological Association Convention, August 31, 1978, Toronto, Canada.

Chapter III

EYEWITNESS TESTIMONY:
LEGAL PERSPECTIVES

INTRODUCTION

PSYCHOLOGY HAS MOUNTED one of its strongest efforts to influence the law in the area of eyewitness testimony (Munsterberg, 1908; Tapp, 1977; Whipple, 1912; Stern, 1939; Whitely and McGeoch, 1927; Freud, 1906; Cady, 1924). In general, however, legal opinions including those rendered by the highest court of the land, the U. S. Supreme Court, provide ample evidence of the fact that there is still a reluctance to give full weight to the scientific findings of behavioral scientists.

The record is somewhat mixed when it comes to the area of eyewitness testimony. In *U.S. v. Wade* (1967), the U. S. Supreme Court adopted a very strong posture in recognizing the serious dangers inherent in eyewitness accounts, yet in *Kirby v. Illinois* (1971) the Court retreated from its earlier stand. In the latter case, the Court concluded that the accused was not entitled to counsel at the arrest stage, despite the fact that he had been identified at a highly prejudicial "showup." *Moore v. State of Illinois* (1977) is a recent example of the highest court's views concerning eyewitness testimony. The majority opinion offered a restatement of earlier expressed opinions concerning the problems of eyewitness identification, but one opinion, offered by Justice Blackmun, still revealed the kind of gross insensitivity to the problem that appears to exist in the minds of many jurists. While concurring in the result, he remarked:

> But ten to fifteen seconds of observation of the face of a rapist at
> midday by his female victim during the commission of the crime by

89

no means is insufficient to leave an accurate and indelible impression
on the victim. One need only observe another person's face for ten
seconds by the clock to know this. To the resisting woman, the ten to
fifteen seconds would seem endless. No female victim of a rape,
given that period of daylight observation, will ever believe otherwise.
(p. 4054)

Blackmun's comments seem to be far more reflective of his
own emotionally biased convictions than the scientific evidence
which is now available to members of the legal community. Any
number of well-designed scientific studies now demonstrate the
gross inaccuracy of many witnesses' reports under circumstances
not unlike those in the *Moore* case (Goldstein, 1977; Buckhout,
1974). There is repeated documentation, both in actual cases
and from experimental evidence, that failings of perception,
memory and reporting create havoc on the validity of testimony
offered. Contrary to Blackmun's implication that the emotional
character of the rape was bound to leave an "indelible impression" on the victim, there is some evidence that the emotional
trauma of the event might have had the opposite effect of shatter-
ing the recall process. Not only is the psychological literature
replete with references to the emotional blocking or amnesia
effects caused by trauma, but it is not uncommon to hear of law
enforcement authorities calling on hypnotists to free up the
memories of victims. These issues were addressed at some length
in the earlier portions of this text.

The accuracy of the eyewitness identification in *Moore* was
rightly treated with skepticism by the majority of Supreme Court
justices. Specifically, the potential suggestiveness and bias of
lineups had been focused on earlier as a major problem in the
Wade - Gilbert - Stovall trilogy. The vacillation offered by the
Court in these different opinions has provided new data for
critics that the Court has not fully grasped the problems associated
with eyewitness accounts. Examined from a different perspective,
the Burger Court has provided an additional illustration of its
reduced concern for defendants' rights in contrast with its pred-
ecessor.

This chapter will present and discuss the major U.S. Supreme
Court opinions that affect eyewitness testimony, including the

attention that has been given to both lineups and photographic identifications. In the concluding portion, the author will offer guidelines for addressing the problem of eyewitness identification, integrating both the psychological as well as legal issues.

THE WADE, GILBERT AND STOVALL OPINIONS

The Supreme Court in Wade (1967) claimed the need for defense counsel's presence at pretrial lineups. The majority stated that this was necessary in order to protect the Sixth Amendment guarantee to the accused's right to counsel not only at his trial, but at any critical confrontation where the results might determine his fate.

Wade was indicted for robbery of a federally insured bank in Eustace, Texas, on September 21, 1964. He was placed in a lineup, without notice to his appointed counsel, with strips of tape placed on his face (as the robber had allegedly done). In addition, upon request, he repeated words like those the robber had allegedly employed during the holdup. Two bank employees later identified Wade in the courtroom during his trial. The defendant claimed that his Fifth Amendment privilege against self-incrimination, along with his Sixth Amendment right to counsel, had been violated. The trial court rejected these motions and Wade was convicted; but the Court of Appeals reversed, holding that there had been no Fifth Amendment violation, but his right to counsel had been improperly denied. The U.S. Supreme Court granted certiorari and the case was argued on February 16, 1967, with the decision being handed down on June 12, 1967.

The majority opinion, offered by Justice Brennan, presented a thorough and critical analysis of the issues involved in eyewitness identification. Only at the trial did defense counsel elicit from the bank employees that their in-court identification of Wade had been preceded by their earlier lineup identification. The Supreme Court's opinion noted that nothing involved in the lineup procedure had violated Wade's privilege against self-incrimination. The Court had just previously stated in *Schmerber v. California* (384 U.S.757, 761) that "the Fifth Amendment protects an accused only from being compelled to testify against himself, or otherwise provide the State with evidence of a testimonial or communicative nature." In general, the Court observed that requiring a person to present his person or utter words was not the same as compelling him to give *testimonial* evidence against himself.

However, concerning Wade's right to counsel, Brennan, arguing for the majority, pointed to the critical nature of the lineup procedure. He stated that the assistance of counsel at the lineup was "indispensable" to protect Wade's most basic right as a criminal defendant, which is to be allowed to cross-examine the witnesses against him to insure a fair trial. Brennan stressed that modern day law enforcement procedures involved critical confrontations of the accused in which his fate might be sealed at the pretrial state, rendering the trial proceedings a formality. The government's case, in which the lineup was likened to other scientific evidence gathering and analysis, including fingerprints, blood samples, clothing, hair, etc., was rejected. The Court rightfully pointed out that these other scientific analyses were open to scrutiny by the other side. Therefore, the presence of defense counsel was not crucial in protecting the accused's right to a fair trial.

At this juncture, the Court's opinion presented the full range of problems inherent in eyewitness identification, citing Wall (1965), Rolph (1962), and others. Sensitive to "face saving" techniques, Brennan, quoting from Williams and Hammelman (1963) offered, "It is a matter of common experience that once a witness has picked out the accused at the lineup, he is not likely to go back on his word later on, so that, in practice, the issue of identity may (in the absence of other relevant evidence) for all practical purposes be determined there and then, before the trial." The obvious problem of a showup (presentation of the suspect alone) was addressed by the Court along with the general problem that lineups cannot be recreated. Wigmore's (1937) suggestion of standardizing the entire procedure through use of "100 talking films" in which men of different races, heights, occupations, etc., would be available was mentioned. In Wigmore's (1937) procedure, twenty-five films would be shown in succession in a special room in which witnesses would press buttons when they wished to make identifications. The hesitation in the identification would be mechanically recorded.

Additional issues, such as the erroneous identification of a suspect due to a victim's outrage and consequent vengefulness were addressed. Furthermore, the Court stated *(United States v. Wade, 1967)*: "Any protestations by the suspect of the fairness of the lineup made at trial are likely to be in vain; the jury's choice is between the accused's unsupported version and that of the police officers present." In *Wade,* counsel elicited from cross-examination that one witness had observed the suspect in the custody of an F.B.I. agent, and another had seen a person in the hall in the custody of the agent who "resembled the person that we identified as the one who had entered the bank."

The notion of an original identification being *bolstered* is presented in the Court's opinion when it states:

> The lineup is most often used as in the present case to crystallize the witnesses' identification of the defendant for future reference. We have already noted that the lineup identification will have that effect. The State may then rest upon the witnesses' unequivocal courtroom identification, and not mention the pretrial identification as part of the State's case at trial. (1939)

The difficulty in determining when an original identification is not subsequently tainted by later viewing of the suspect in lineups, photoarrays, pretrial hearing, etc., is presented by Justice Black in a dissenting opinion. He noted that the majority opinion required that the case be remanded for "a hearing to determine whether the in-court identification had an independent source." He states:

> I think it is practically impossible. How is a witness capable of probing the recesses of his mind to draw a sharp line between a courtroom identification due exclusively to an earlier lineup and a courtroom identification due to memory not based on the lineup? What kind of "clear and convincing evidence" can the prosecution offer to prove upon what particular events memories resulting in an in-court identification rest? (1943)

The Supreme Court presented a new *per se* rule in offering the *Wade* opinion. Essentially, the rule as cited by Justice White, in his dissenting opinion, is as follows:

> A criminal suspect cannot be subjected to a pretrial identification

process in the absence of his counsel without violating the Sixth Amendment. If he is, the State may not buttress a later court-room identification of the witness by any reference to the previous identification. Furthermore, the courtroom identification is not admissible at all unless the State can establish by clear and convincing proof that the testimony is not the fruit of the earlier identification made in the absence of defendant's counsel—admittedly a heavy burden for the State and probably an impossible one. To all intent and purposes, courtroom identifications are barred if pretrial identifications have occurred without counsel being present. (p. 1944)

The Gilbert Opinion

In *Gilbert* (1967) the defendant was convicted of armed robbery and the murder of a police officer. He alleged that constituional error occurred in the admission of testimony of some of the witnesses who had identified him at a lineup which occurred sixteen days after his indictment and after the appointment of counsel. His attorney was not notified of the lineup. Furthermore, the "petitioner" claimed constitutional errors occurred in the admission of handwriting exemplars taken from him after his arrest and in the admission of a co-defendant's out-of-court statements that implicated him. Finally, he claimed that his Fourth Amendment rights were violated by police seizure of photographs of him from his locked apartment after a warrantless entry, including the subsequent admission of testimony identifying him from these photographs.

For the purpose of addressing the problem of eyewitness testimony, a number of the above-mentioned issues are of little interest. The U. S. Supreme Court ruled that the taking of "handwriting exemplars" did not violate the petitioner's Fifth Amendment privileges against self-incrimination. Justice Brennan, writing for the majority stated:

> The privilege reaches only compulsion of an accused's communications, whatever form they might take, and the compulsion of responses which are also communications, for example, compliance with a subpoena to produce one's papers, and not "compulsion which makes a suspect or accused the source of real or physical evidence . . . . "*Schmerber v. California* 384 U.S. 757, 763-764. One's voice and handwriting are, of course, means of communication. It by no means follows, however, that every compulsion of an accused to use

his voice or write compels a communication within the cover of the privilege. A mere handwriting exemplar, in contrast to the content of what is written, like the voice or body itself, is an identifying physical characteristic outside its protection. (p. 1953)

Gilbert contended that admission of a co-defendant's statements violated his right to due process of law, but the Court, after offering a brief rationale for its position, chose "not to pass on this contention." Regarding Gilbert's claim that photographs were illegally seized, the Court decided that "the facts do not appear with sufficient clarity to decide that question," and therefore vacated certiorari.

Since the Court failed to offer "relief" on these issues, the question of the in-court identification and lineup identifications became critical as they related to the companion ruling in *United States v. Wade* (1967).

Three eyewitnesses who identified Gilbert at the trial had observed him at a lineup conducted without notice to his counsel sixteen days after his indictment and appointment of his attorney. The lineup took place in a Los Angeles auditorium on a stage behind bright lights. Approximately 100 persons were in the audience, each an eyewitness to one of several robberies (not merely the one in Alhambra which was addressed in this case) that Gilbert was alleged to have committed. The opinion of the Court of Appeals for the Ninth Circuit offered a number of details concerning what took place at the lineup. Approximately ten to thirteen prisoners were placed on the stage. The witnesses were in a darkened portion of the stage. The Ninth Circuit Court opinion included the following descriptive statement *(Gilbert v. United States,* 1967).

> Each man in the lineup was identified by number, but not by name. Each man was required to step forward into a marked circle, to turn, presenting both profiles as well as a face and back view, to walk, to put on or take off certain articles of clothing. When a man's number was called and he was directed to step into the circle, he was asked certain questions: where he was picked up, whether he owned a car, whether, when arrested, he was armed, where he lived. Each was also asked to repeat certain phrases, both in a loud and in a soft voice, phrases that witnesses to the crimes had heard the robbers use: "Freeze, this is a stickup; this is a holdup; empty your cash

drawer; this is a heist; don't anybody move." Either while the men
were on the stage, or after they were taken from it, it is not clear
which, the assembled witnesses were asked if there were any that
they would like to see again, and told that if they had doubts, now
was the time to resolve them. Several gave the numbers of men
they wanted to see, including Gilbert's. While the other prisoners
were no longer present, Gilbert and two or three others were again
put through a similar procedure. Some of the witnesses asked that a
particular prisoner say a particular phrase, or walk a particular way.
After the lineup, the witnesses talked to each other; it is not clear
that they did so during the lineup. They did, however, in each
other's presence, call out the numbers of men they could identify.
(p. 1955)

*The mere fact that witnesses called out numbers of individuals
they identified was overwhelmingly prejudicial to those identified.*
One could hardly arrange a lineup that would be more prejudicial. While the Court does not and could not specifically document conversations that took place during the lineup, undoubtedly there were numerous conversations among the observers.
With as many as 100 people in the auditorium viewing the lineup,
the possible contaminating effects of responses (both verbal and
nonverbal) would be myriad, given the potential network of
interaction.

A further description of the events involved in this case is
available from Justice Brennan's opinion. At the "guilt stage,"
one witness (a cashier) offered an in-court identification, but defense counsel moved, out of the presence of the jury, to strike her
testimony on the ground that she had identified Gilbert at the
pretrial lineup in which defense counsel was not present. This
motion was denied by the trial judge. The defense lawyer also
elicited the fact of lineup identifications from two other eyewitnesses who on direct examination identified Gilbert in the
courtroom. Also, at the "penalty stage," Gilbert's defense attorney objected to the testimony of eight witnesses to other robberies who had identified him earlier at the lineup.

As in *Wade,* the Court ruled that the admission of in-court
identifications without first determining that they were not
"tainted" by the illegal lineup but were of independent origin
was constitutional error. However, the Court also stated, as they

had in *Wade,* that the record does not permit an informed judgment whether the in-court identifications at the two stages (guilt and penalty) of the trial had an *independent* source. Therefore, the Court noted that Gilbert was entitled only to a vacation of his conviction pending the possible holding of proceedings in California Supreme Court on this matter. The reader should note that the California Court, of course, was free to decide whether or not to use the opportunity to establish an *independent source.*

Different issues were involved as to the admission of the testimony of the manager of the apartment house at the guilt phase and of the eight witnesses at the penalty stage. Here Justice Brennan, once again, writing for the majority, notes:

> Testimony is the direct result of the illegal lineup 'come at by exploitation of [the primary] illegality.' *Wong Sun v. United States,* 371 U.S. 471,488. The State is therefore not entitled to an opportunity to show that that testimony had an independent source. Only a *per se* exclusionary rule as to such testimony can be an effective sanction to assume that law enforcement authorities will respect the accused's constitutional right to the presence of his counsel at the critical lineup. In the absence of legislative regulations adequate to avoid the hazards to a fair trial which inhere in lineups as presently conducted, the desirability of deterring the constitutionally objectionable practice must prevail over the undesirability of excluding relevant evidence. (p. 1957)

Thus, in the majority opinion, the Court presented an exclusionary rule designed to limit abuses associated with eyewitness identification lineups. The presence of defense counsel was deemed to be mandatory. Some legal scholars believed this to be strong medicine to counter bias and prejudices in this area, and commentary offered from law reviews will be cited later in support of this view. Also, the Supreme Court's opinion in *Stovall v. Denno, Warden,* 388 U.S., 293, shed further light on their view of the exclusionary rule.

The Stovall Opinion

In *Stovall v. Denno, Warden* (1967), the Supreme Court ruled on the question of whether or not their *Wade* and *Gilbert* opinions would be retroactively applied to *Stovall.* In addition, the question of whether or not Stovall was denied due process of law

(Fourteenth Amendment) was considered. Stovall was convicted of murdering a Dr. Behrendt about midnight in the kitchen of his home in Garden City, Long Island, on August 23, 1961. His wife followed the assailant into the kitchen and "jumped" at him, but he knocked her down and stabbed her eleven times. The police later found a shirt with keys in the pocket which they traced to the defendant.

Mrs. Behrendt was hospitalized for major surgery, and the police, without allowing Stovall time to retain counsel, brought the defendant to the victim's hospital room to be viewed. She was asked if he "was the man" and after he was directed to utter a "few words for voice identification;" positive recognition was given. At the trial, the police officers and Mrs. Behrendt testified to the hospital room identification and an in-court identification was also offered by the victim. Stovall was committed and sentenced to death. The case eventually reached the U. S. Supreme Court.

In this case, the Supreme Court's opinion stated that the *Wade* and *Gilbert* rulings applied only to those cases and future cases and that the requirement of counsel's presence at confrontations for identification purposes could not be applied retroactively to this case.

While acknowledging the potential bias and prejudice associated with the one-on-one confrontation arranged between the witness and the defendant in her hospital room, the Supreme Court's majority opinion speaks to the urgency of the situation and the "totality of the circumstances surrounding it," in affirming the Court of Appeals, *en banc,* 355 F. 2nd at 735.

> Here was the only person in the world who could possibly exonerate Stovall. Her words, and only her words, "He is not the man" could have resulted in freedom for Stovall. The hospital was not far distant from the courthouse and jail. No one knew how long Mrs. Behrendt might live. Faced with the responsibility of identifying the attacker, with the need for immediate action and with the knowledge that Mrs. Behrendt could not visit the jail, the police followed the only feasible procedure and took Stovall to the hospital room. Under these circumstances the usual police station lineup, which Stovall now argues he should have had, was out of the question. (p. 1972)

While the court went to great lengths in *Wade* to emphasize the importance of fairness in eyewitness identification, it decided in *Stovall* that if sufficient urgency arose that required an immediate encounter between victim and suspect, the earlier cautions could be cast aside. Among the dissenters, however, Justice Fortas would reverse and remand for a new trial on the ground that the State's reference at trial to the improper hospital identification violated petitioner's Fourteenth Amendment rights and was prejudicial." (p. 303) Justice Black, in another dissenting opinion, pointed to the problem of relying on "the totality of circumstances." He stated:

> The concept of due process under which the Court purports to decide this question, however, is that this Court looks at "the totality of the circumstances" of a particular case to determine in its own judgment whether they comport with the Court's notions of decency, fairness, and fundamental justice, and, if so, declares they comport with the Constitution, and, if not, declares they are forbidden by the Constitution. See, e.g. *Rochin v. California,* 342 U.S. 165. Such a constitutional formula substitutes this Court's judgment of what is right for what the Constitution declares shall be the supreme law of the land. (p. 305)

The trilogy of *Wade-Gilbert-Stovall* created a stir both in the legal community and in the scientific community. Behavioral scientists took particular note of these developments. Before proceding with a discussion of more recent cases such as *Kirby v. Illinois* (1971) and *Moore v. Illinois* (1977) some commentary on these three celebrated cases will be offered.

One law review, the *Columbia Journal of Law and Social Problems,* summarized developments over the three year period since the Supreme Court had offered its landmark rulings. The journal noted that a number of State court rulings in the wake of *Wade* et al. had applied different standards. While a defense lawyer's presence at a pretrial lineup was somehow designed to prevent undue suggestiveness and bias from creeping into the proceedings, they noted that his role was never spelled out. As a result, police departments and courts developed a wide variety of regulations.

The vagueness of "totality of the circumstances" as a criterion in applying the due process test of the Fourteenth Amendment again resulted in a great variety of approaches by judges at the trial level. The authors of this article "Protection of the Accused at Police Lineups," concluded that "upgrading of pretrial identification procedures is not likely to be achieved by the case-by-case determination of the courts as to what procedures violate due process" (354). Therefore, the commentators went on to present a model set of regulations that they believed, if adopted by legislatures, would insure fair and accurate pretrial procedures.

As evidence of the variability in lineup procedures that were created in the wake of *Wade,* the authors cited a survey undertaken by their journal. In drawing on responses from fifty-six police departments, the journal noted that in thirty-eight departments, lawyers were allowed to "merely watch," while in seven, they were allowed to "suggest procedure." In three instances, lawyers were allowed to suggest procedure and question witnesses" and in three other departments, lawyers could "suggest procedure and make objections."

In discussing the role of lawyers in lineups in response to *Wade,* Levine and Tapp (1973) noted that they might even be harmful by lending an appearance of legitimacy to them. While the Supreme Court sought to remedy biasing effects at postindictment lineups by requiring the presence of counsel, the regulations —and particularly who should draw them up—appeared to be a central issue according to these authors. The previously mentioned survey of police departments' varied approaches to the problem helps support their view.

Sobel (1972) in his work, *Eye-Witness Identification: Legal and Practical Problems,* has attempted to place the impact of *Wade-Gilbert-Stovall* in perspective. He states:

Although *Wade-Gilbert-Stovall* are important decisions, they do not affect a substantial number of trials [about 5 percent from my own empirical investigation]. The key to this observation is that the decisions are concerned with in-court eyewitness testimony but only in those cases where the police had arranged a pretrial confrontation between the eyewitness and the defendant for the purpose of establishing identity. In short, the decisions apply to those crimes where the police had found it necessary to establish identity of the perpetrator by means of lineup or a showup or by photo identification procedures (p. 4).

The Kirby Opinion

Kirby v. Illinois (1971) is a case in which a man by the name of Willie Shard claimed to have been robbed by two men on a Chicago street. The day after the robbery was reported, police stopped two individuals (including a Ralph Bean, as well as Kirby) who possessed items that had been reported stolen by Shard, including some personal items of identification. The relationship between the items and Shard, however, was not discovered until Kirby and Bean were taken to the police station. As soon as the determination had been made, a police car was dispatched to pick up Shard and bring him to the police station. As soon as he arrived at the police station, the victim was brought into a room where the two suspects were seated. He immediately offered a positive identification of the two men. No lawyer was present nor had either of the suspects been advised as to their right of counsel. Neither had asked for an attorney's assistance. At the trial, Shard was a witness for the prosecution and he reported on his earlier identifications. An earlier pretrial motion to suppress Shard's identification testimony was denied. Both defendants were found guilty at the trial and an appeal to the Illinois Appellate Court failed. Finally, the U.S. Supreme Court affirmed the lower court rulings, and it emphasized that Kirby did not have a right to counsel at the arrest stage, nor at the point before the initiation of any adversary criminal proceeding. In presenting the plurality opinion, Justice Stewart stated:

> In a line of constitutional cases in this Court stemming back to the Court's landmark opinion in *Powell v. Alabama*, 128 U.S. 45, it has been firmly established that a person's Sixth and Fourteenth Amendment right to counsel attached only at or after the time that adversary judicial proceedings have been initiated against him. See *Powell v. Alabama, supra; Johnson v. Zerbst*, 304 U.S. 458; *Hamilton v. Alabama*, 368 U.S. 52; *Gideon v. Wainwright*, 372 U.S. 335; *White v. Maryland*, 373 U.S. 59; *Massiah v. United States*, 377 U.S. 201; *United States v. Wade*, 388 U.S. 218; *Gilbert v. California*, 388 U.S. 263; *Coleman v. Alabama*, 399 U.S. 1. This is not that a defendant in a criminal case has constitutional right to counsel only at the trial

itself. The *Powell* case makes clear that the right attaches at the time of arraignment and the Court has recently held that it exists also at the time of a preliminary hearing, *Coleman v. Alabama, Supra.* But the point is that, while members of the Court have differed as to existence of the right to counsel in the contexts of some of the above cases, *all* of those cases have involved points of time at or after the initiation of adversary judicial criminal proceedings—whether by way of formal charge, preliminary hearing, indictment, or arraignment. (p. 1882)

Somewhat later, Stewart continues:

The initiation of judicial criminal proceedings is far from a mere formalism. It is the starting point of our whole system of adversary criminal justice. For it is only then that the government has committed itself to prosecute, and only then that the adverse positions of government and defendant have solidified. It is then that a defendant finds himself faced with the prosecutorial forces of organized society, and immersed in the intricacies of substantive procedural criminal law. (p. 1882)

Thus, Stewart, writing for the plurality, relies on what he perceives as solid support from previous cases to support his position. Furthermore, he draws a sharp line between the arrest stage and the point at which the State initiates "judicial criminal proceedings." Is this an artificial line for purposes of determining prejudice directed against the defendant? Justice Brennan in a dissenting opinion believes so when he states:

While it should go without saying, it appears necessary in view of the plurality opinion today, to reemphasize that Wade did not require the presence of counsel at pretrial confrontations for identification purposes simply on the basis of an abstract consideration of the words "criminal prosecutions" in the Sixth Amendment. Counsel is required at those confrontations because "the dangers inherent in eyewitness identification and the suggestibility inherent in the context of the pretrial identification, *"id,* at 235, mean that protection must be afforded to the 'most basic right [of] a criminal defendant—his right to a fair trial at which the witnesses against him might be meaningfully cross-examined," *id,* at 224. Indeed, the court expressly stated that "legislative or other regulations, such as those of local police departments which eliminate the risks of abuse and unintentional suggestion at lineup proceedings and the impediments to meaningful confrontation at trial may also remove the basis for regarding the stage as critical." *Id.,* at 239; see id., at 239 n. 30; *Gilbert v California,* 388 U.S. at 273. Hence, "the initiation of adversary judicial criminal proceedings," *ante* at 689, is completely irrelevant to whether counsel is necessary at a pretrial confrontation for identification in order to safeguard the accused's constitutional rights to confrontation and the effective assistance of counsel at his trial.

In view of *Wade,* it is plain, and the plurality today does not attempt to dispute it, that there inhere in a confrontation for identification conducted after arrest the identical hazards to a fair trial that inhere in such a confrontation conducted "after the onset of formal prosecutorial proceedings," *Id.,* at 690. The plurality apparently considers an arrest, which for present purposes we must assume to be based upon probable cause, to be nothing more than part of "a routine police investigation," *ibid.,* and thus not "the starting point of our whole system of adversary criminal justice." (p. 1886)

The context of the encounter between Shard and the defendants does appear to provide an excellent setting for prejudice and bias. Undoubtedly angry at the loss of personal items, Shard was brought to the police station and offered two individuals for viewing, both being in the custody of police officers. These circumstances were designed to encourage an identification(s) regardless of the guilt or innocence of the parties.

Photographic Identification

Writing in the English publication, *The Criminal Law Review, Williams and Hammelman* (1963) clearly stated a major problem in the use of photographs:

Equally serious can be the effect of showing a photograph of a particular suspect to a witness with the question whether he recognizes the man, if the same witness is afterwards to be confronted with this man at the parade. Subsequent identification of the accused then shows nothing except that the picture was a good likeness. The same objection applies, though in reduced degree, where the witness has actually picked out this particular man from a whole series of photographs. Even the mere issue of a photograph or Identi-kit picture of a wanted suspect, to the press or on T.V., may create a prejudice against a possibly innocent man. (p. 484)

While scholars generally seem to agree that photo identifications are unreliable, the Supreme Court in *Simmons* (Sobel, 1972) argued that the unreliability factor could be minimized by virtue of the cross-examination available to counsel. Specifically, they stated in this 1968 case *(Simmons v. United States,* 390 U.S. 377) :

> We are unwilling to prohibit its employment, either in the exercise of our supervisory power or, still less, as a matter of constitutional requirement. Instead, we hold that each case must be considered on its own facts, and that convictions based on eyewitness identification at trial following a pretrial identification by photograph will be set aside on that ground only if the photographic identification procedure was so impermissibly suggestive as to give rise to a very substantial likelihood of irreparable misidentification. (p. 46)

Sobel (1972) has pointed out that while the Supreme Court offered the above opinion in conjunction with its decision involving the use of a photographic identification during the *investigative* stage, no mention was made of the role of photographic identification at the *custody* or *defendant* stages.

Neil v. Biggers (1972), 409 U.S. 188, however, attempted to further clarify the Court's view of eyewitness identifications. In this case, the victim was raped by the accused who first approached her in the doorway to her kitchen. After a brief struggle, she was walked at knifepoint to about two blocks from her home and raped on a moonlit evening. The entire episode she claimed took place between 15 and 30 minutes. She gave police a general description of the man as "fat and flabby with smooth skin, bushy hair and a youthful voice." She also claimed to have offered that he was between sixteen and eighteen years of age, around 5 feet, 10 inches tall and weighed between 180 and 200 pounds. Several times over the ensuing months, she viewed suspects in lineups or in showups and was shown between thirty and forty photographs. She stated that one of the men pictured in one of of the photographs had similar features to those of her assailant but identified none of the suspects.

On August 17, after making a hurried, unsuccessful attempt to get "standins" for a lineup, the victim was called to the courthouse where she was shown a single suspect who was held by two police officers. She claimed she had no doubt about this person and identified him. Later, in court, she stated, "I have no doubt, I mean that I am sure that when—see, when I first laid eyes on him, I knew that it was the individual, because his face—well, there was just something that I don't think I could ever forget. I believe . . . ." She explained further, after being questioned, that "first laid eyes on him" meant the identification in the courthouse.

As part of the opinion in *Neil v. Biggers* (1972)), the Court offered guidelines to be considered in weighing the possible suggestiveness of some identifications versus the need to generally rely on them as a technique for law enforcement. They include the witness' opportunity to view the criminal at the time of the crime, the witness' degree of attention, the accuracy of his prior description of the criminal, the level of certainty demonstrated at the confrontation, and the time between the crime and the confrontation.

In *U. S. v. Ash* (1973), the Court held that the Sixth Amendment did "not require that defense counsel be present when a witness views police or prosecution photographic arrays." Furthermore the Court pointed out that these showings, unlike corporeal identifications, are not trial like adversarial confrontations and therefore "no possibility arises that the accused might be misled by his lack of familiarity with the law or overpowered by his professional adversary." In this opinion, the Court also noted that the defense counsel had an equal chance to prepare for trial by presenting his own photographic displays to witnesses before trial and that "duplication by defense counsel is a safeguard that normally is not available when a formal confrontation occurs."

Here is another instance in which the Court is inconsistent with its other rulings on eyewitness identifications. They offer a very low standard in *Ash,* demonstrating a gross insensitivity to the potential prejudice and bias associated with the presentation of photographic arrays. While the Supreme Court has placed great emphasis on the point or "stage" of proceedings at which identifications occur, the reality is that an eyewitness identification may be just as harmful at an early stage (arrest) as at a later stage (pretrial). Likewise, any photographic array may be extremely prejudicial, as Buckhout (1974) has demonstrated. The notion that defense counsel may present its own arrays does not offset the potentially prejudicial impact of a biased array presented by law enforcement authorities. *It appears that too often the courts*

*view the adversarial system as an adequate safeguard when in fact
there is little empirical evidence to support their views.* In
general, the scientific community's disagreements with the Courts
appear to be very strong on this issue.

The Court returned to these criteria when they reversed a
Court of Appeals ruling in Connecticut. The case, *John R.
Manson v. Brathwaite,* (1977), is reported in Uviller (1977). In
this case, an undercover police officer purchased heroin from a
seller through the open doorway of an apartment. His observation was for several minutes in a hallway illuminated by natural
light. A very specific description of the seller was then passed on
to another officer who then produced a photograph at a later
point. The undercover officer, Glover, identified Brathwaite as
the seller.

At the trial, some eight months later, the photograph was received in evidence and Glover made a positive identification of
the defendant in court. Later, after the Connecticut Supreme
Court affirmed the conviction, Brathwaite filed a petition for
habeas corpus in Federal District Court alleging that the admission of the identification testimony violated the Fourteenth
Amendment (Due Process). The Court ruled that the "totality
of circumstances" discussed in *Stovall v. Denno* (1967) should be
considered. While acknowledging the suggestiveness of the identification, they pointed out counterbalancing factors: "the witness' opportunity to view the criminal at the time of the crime,
the witness' degree of attention, the accuracy of his prior description of the criminal, the level of certainty demonstrated at the
confrontation, and the time between the crime and the confrontation" (p. 41). Thus, in a seven to two decision, the Appeals
Court was reversed and Brathwaite's earlier conviction upheld.

As mentioned in the earlier section on photo identification,
one can never be certain if it is the original observation or the
subsequent photo identification or a later lineup or showup, or a
combination of these that the witness is responding to. Sobel
(1978) states that cross-examination is an adequate safeguard only
if counsel was present at the moment of identification and can
therefore bring out the bias or suggestiveness that was present on
the earlier occasion.

The author cannot agree with Sobel. There are so many conditions under which distortion and bias may interfere with accurate eyewitness identification, that cross-examination, with or without counsel's presence "at the moment of identification," is hardly sufficient to insure the integrity of the process.

The Moore Opinion

Moore (Moore v. Illinois, 1977) raised questions involving the interpretation of earlier U.S. Supreme Court opinions presented in *Wade, Gilbert,* and *Kirby.* In this case, the victim awakened from a nap to find a man standing in her doorway with a knife in his hand. She was thrown down on the bed by her assailant and after partly covering his face with a bandana, forced her to commit oral sodomy. The attacker then raped her and left, taking a guitar and flute from her apartment. While she had only seen his face briefly (perhaps ten to fifteen seconds during the attack), she stated that she thought he was the same man who had made offensive remarks to her in a neighborhood bar on the previous evening.

During the following week, the victim was shown two groups of photographs, one group of 200 and a second group of ten. From the first group, she selected about thirty who resembled her assailant in height, weight, and build. From the second group of ten, she selected two or three. One of these was the defendant. Police also found a letter in the notebook that the victim had given them. An investigation noted that it belonged to a woman with whom the defendant had been staying.

One of the most important aspects of the case involved the confrontation between the victim and the accused *(Moore v. Illinois,* 1977) :

> The next morning, a policeman accompanied the victim to a Cook County Municipal Court for the hearing. The policeman told her she was going to view a suspect and should identify him if she could. He also had her sign a complaint that named petitioner as her assailant. At the hearing, petitioner's name was called and he was led before the bench. The judge told petitioner that he was charged with rape and deviate sexual behavior. The judge then called the victim, who had been in the courtroom waiting for the case to be called, to come before the bench. The State's attorney stated that police had found evidence linking petitioner with the offenses charged. He asked the

victim whether she saw her assailant in the courtroom, and she pointed at petitioner. (p. 4051)

At a later hearing, the accused was bound over to the grand jury which indicted him for rape, deviate sexual behavior, burglary and robbery. An attorney was appointed and he moved to suppress the identification on the basis of its suggestiveness, and the fact that counsel had not been present. At an evidentiary hearing, the Court rejected this motion on the grounds that the prosecution had demonstrated an "independent basis" for the identification.

At the trial, the defendant was found guilty on all four counts. He was sentenced and later the Illinois Supreme Court affirmed the conviction. Again, the "independent basis" of the identification was cited by the Court. After the U.S. Supreme Court denied certiorari, the petitioner sought a writ of habeas corpus from the Federal District Court indicating that both his Sixth and Fourteenth Amendment rights were violated. The Court of Appeals for the Seventh Circuit affirmed and the U. S. Supreme court granted certiorari.

The majority opinion reviewed some of the earlier problems associated with eyewitness accounts and presented in *Wade, Gilbert,* and *Kirby.* The sources of bias and weaknesses inherent in eyewitness identifications were noted. In applying the rationale from these earlier rulings, the Court pointed to the fact that counsel had not been present at the preliminary hearing at which time the victim had offered the identification. In addition, the prosecution introduced evidence of the identification at the trial as part of its case-in-chief.

While the Court of Appeals argued that *Wade* and *Gilbert* did not apply in this case because the in-court identification could hardly be considered a lineup, the Supreme Court opinion noted that the basic problem of bias and prejudice cited in those cases clearly did apply to *Moore.* They stated:

> Indeed, a one-on-one confrontation generally is thought to present greater risks of mistaken identification than a lineup. E.g., P. Wall, Eye-Witness Identification in Criminal Cases, 27-40 (1965); Williams and Hammelman. (1965), Identification Parades, Part I, (1963), Criminal Law Review 480-481. There is no reason, then, to hold

that a one-on-one identification procedure is not subject to the same requirements as a lineup. (p. 4053)

Further along in the opinion, the Court added:

It is difficult to imagine a more suggestive manner in which to present a suspect to a witness for their critical first confrontation than was employed in this case. The victim, who had seen her assailant for only ten to fifteen seconds, was asked to make her identification after she was told that she was going to view a suspect, after she was told his name and heard it called as he was led before the bench, and after she heard the prosecutor recite the evidence believed to implicate petitioner. Had petitioner been represented by counsel, some or all of this suggestiveness could have been avoided. (p. 1053)

The Supreme Court's opinion went on to state that Moore's right to counsel (Sixth Amendment) had been clearly violated, and citing *Gilbert* observed that the prosecution was not entitled to show that the testimony had an "independent source" because "that testimony is the direct result of the illegal lineup come at by exploitation of [the primary] illegality."

Finally, the Court stated that because of "the violation of petitioner's Sixth and Fourteenth Amendment right to counsel at the pretrial corporeal identification, and of the prosecution's exploitation at trial of evidence derived directly from that violation, we reverse the judgment of the Court of Appeals and remand for a determination of whether the failure to exclude that evidence was harmless constitutional error under *Chapman v. California,* 386 U.S. 18 (1967) " (p. 4054).

In the previous chapter, the author quoted from Justice Blackmun's concurring opinion in which he "disassociated" himself from the view that there was something insignificant or unreliable about the rape victim's eyewitness testimony. Therefore, the matter will not be reviewed again.

While demonstrating a rather deep awareness of the usual problems associated with eyewitness testimony, greater attention might have been placed on the problem of the use of photos in this case. It is entirely possible that the victim's choice of two or three photos (which included Moore) from among the second group of thirty that she viewed resulted in a mistaken courtroom identification. The Court's lack of sensitivity to the strong potential for bias and prejudice associated with the use of photographic arrays was nowhere more clearly demonstrated than in the *Ash* case. *Police and prosecutors are free to present photos in any manner they choose, and defense counsel is not required to be present.*

In *Moore,* it could be argued that the victim was uncertain about the identity of her assailant as she was unable to *single him out,* but merely included his photo from among several she selected. Then, later on, she was presented with the highly prejudicial showing of him in court (a "showup") and identified him, but this identification may have been contaminated as a result of her selection of his photo. Thus, the historical problem which Wall (1965) so eloquently described is presented: did the victim recall a face as a result of the original perception of the person or as a result of viewing his photo?

As reported earlier, Buckhout, Figueroa, and Hoff (1975) demonstrated that merely tilting a photo, along with presentation of a different facial expression, were sufficient to cause it to be more frequently selected in an array.

A FRAMEWORK FOR MORE ACCURATE EYEWITNESS IDENTIFICATION

As a result of the problems addressed in these initial chapters, it becomes evident that while sensitivity to this issue has grown over the years, particularly in the courts, it is still necessary that reforms be instituted. A number of writers have offered suggestions and have raised questions in this area, including Buckout (1974), Levine and Tapp (1973), LaSota (1974) and Goldstein (1977). Buckhout's (1974) analysis of the "source of unreliability" is particularly helpful. It should be ready by any serious student of eyewitness testimony.

In summary, there are a number of issues which I wish to highlight in this closing section on eyewitness testimony.

The eyewitness account is certainly one of the main points whether or not it takes the form of stereotyping, blatant prejudice, a desire to be helpful to the police, or, as Buckhout (1974) states, a desire to be a part of history. All human beings view the world in their own unique even idiosyncratic manner; no one escapes the biasing impact of social development.

Selectiveness in perception is also inextricably interwoven with this general approach. Our experiences tend to shape the growth process in curious ways, and as a result, we unconsciously tend to block out certain phenomena while tuning into other stimuli. Some events strike us as more critical and deserving of our attention while others seem uninteresting if not irrelevant. However, even those events which rivet our attention may be overwhelming and thus impact negatively on our ability to recall them.

Certainly, factors that are imbedded in the situation itself have an impact no matter how unbiased and attentive the eyewitness. The speed of events and the opportunity for a clear, unobstructed view must be considered, particularly given the fact that it is unusual when an eyewitness would be afforded excellent viewing conditions. The potentially serious problems inherent in eyewitness testimony as a function of police behavior and in response to both obvious and subtle expectations of lineup administrators are obvious. The law and the expression it takes in the form of the behavior of the functionaries—police, judge, lawyers and others—are part of the stimulus situation and independent of observer characteristics. The problems of delays in court proceedings and the frequent cancellation of lineups as a function of "game playing" and manipulative tactics on the part of attorneys affect the memories of eyewitnesses in negative ways. Often this works to the advantage of the defendant.

Any number of additional points, including those incorporated in the "Model Rules" (LaSota, 1974), have been presented by other writers. A number of written pieces that emphasize the legal aspects of the problem have been presented in law review articles; several were cited earlier. Concerning rules, the reader may recall Goldstein's (1977) earlier caution that eyewitness reports, uncorroborated by additional evidence, should not be admitted into evidence. His position is obviously a strong one concerning the problems and weaknesses associated with eyewitness accounts, and has some drawbacks associated with it, given the absolute nature of it.

In synthesizing the extensive material that bears on the problem of eyewitness testimony, the author has repeatedly found himself considering the role of police. I believe that Levine and Tapp (1973) were correct in emphasizing this as an issue in terms of the potential *bias of the police personnel* who make arrests. An officer who makes an arrest has a vested interest in the process and he should not be allowed to conduct the lineup which includes the suspect he has apprehended.

While this problem appears to be a significant one, it poses what appears to be a serious problem in terms of an alternative solution. Police have been charged with the responsibility associated with the apprehension and arrest of criminal offenders. They are the key functionaries in the investigatory stage of the criminal justice process. While the author is tempted to recommend that individuals who are disassociated with the apprehension and arrest process be charged with conducting lineups, that appears to be too unwieldy, particularly for medium-sized or small police agencies. Even if this were possible, police communicate among themselves and contamination might occur.

One obvious reform poses itself in this field as it does in many others—the need for consistency and uniformity in procedures, particularly as they impact upon reliability. There is a great lack in the *uniformity* of procedures used to conduct lineups. While the U. S. Supreme Court opinions have been helpful in pointing to the larger issues, the Court's views have not clearly established guidelines. A number of law review articles have described the uncertainty and chaos that emerged in the wake of the *Wade-Gilbert-Stovall* trilogy. While requiring the presence of defense counsel at lineups conducted at critical stages, their activities and duties were never spelled out by the Court. Later Court opinions have not been helpful in clarifying this point. Documents such as the Police Foundation/Arizona State *Model Rules for Law Enforcement: Eyewitness Identification* represent an attempt to provide guidance for law enforcement personnel and attorneys, but it is questionable how influential such nonmandatory approaches are.

To date, attempts at generating *valid tests for eyewitnesses* have not been fruitful. The reader may recall Goldstein's (1978) empirically based study in which he was interested in seeing if a "morning after" type of test could be useful. He stated that, in general, consistency in facial recognition was too weak to predict future recognitions and therefore a test did not appear feasible.

It is interesting that one can go all the way to Wigmore's (1927) suggestion of "talking films" to find a concept that has merit today. As Wigmore noted in this classic, *The Science of Judicial Proof*, "Some such scientific use of the talking film would go far to reduce the risk of error hitherto inherent in such proceedings (p. 541). While not advocating the creation of a library of 100 "talking films," the modern day application of videotape to this situation would be ideal. Videotape is relatively inexpensive and a large library of tapes could be stored in some central location, perhaps the F.B.I.'s training facility in Virginia. These would be available in very important cases. Smaller numbers of tapes could be distributed to both large and small police agencies throughout America.

The problem of *uniformity*, mentioned earlier, at least as far as the presentation of lineup participants is concerned, is addressed in this approach. After "taping" the suspect, his tape could be integrated easily among tapes of individuals who at least vaguely resemble him. As most scholars and practitioners have noted, the primary task is to include decoys who do not distract noticeably from the suspect.

Wall (1965), Buckhout (1974) and other scholars have pointed to a frequent problem of lineups: too often "stand-ins" are included who look nothing like the suspect. Buckhout (1977) has described a lineup in which a black suspect appeared with all white "stand-ins." A library of videotapes, employing a computerized selection system, would allow for tapes of persons who meet this general criterion to be included. For instance, concerning matters of race, sex, age, height, weight, facial hair, etc., a "search" by a computer could identify tapes of persons who are at least not grossly dissimilar on the above-mentioned characteristics. Ideally, one is not trying to include exact "look-alikes" or "clones," but merely individuals whose outstanding characteristics are not so different from the suspect's that he becomes the obvious target to a lineup observer.

Another important advantage of this approach is that given

the easy *accessibility* to the tapes, "taped lineups" could be run
quickly. Law enforcement authorities who frequently cite the
need for the immediacy of an eyewitness confrontation with the
suspect, and who therefore use "accidental" encounters and "showups," would have no justification for employing such highly prejudicial tactics. Even at 3 A.M., a taped lineup could be run.

While the problems inherent in videotaped lineups would be
less significant than those presented by a photographic array,
corporeal identification procedures would still be preferred
where practicable. Frankly, research would have to be conducted
to document this assertion, but the author believes strongly that
videotaped lineups would demonstrate their superiority to photographic arrays. A victim or eyewitness, if given the opportunity
to observe the suspect in the "flesh and blood" among other carefully selected lineup participants, will be able to engage in a more
valid and meaningful process than if offered a videotaped version.
No matter how advanced the photographic or filming process becomes, it could never be argued that it would be superior to
presenting the person himself. The problem, of course, is that
in actual practice few corporeal identification procedures come
even close to offering lineups with decoys that resemble the
suspect.

Even in a large city like New York, I have observed lineup
authorities desperately searching for "stand-ins" moments before
the lineup was to be conducted. In smaller municipalities and
towns, the problem of obtaining "stand-ins" or decoys who even
remotely resemble the suspect must be very great indeed.

Also, beyond this problem, the whole matter of "coaching"
the "stand-ins" to present themselves in a uniform manner is a
serious one. Different mannerisms, facial expressions, gaits,
clothing, etc. may easily prejudice the lineup observer. Videotaped lineups can reasonably control for these variations. Common sense suggests that a serious problem is presented by the
fact that inexperienced law enforcement personnel are asked to
supervise lineups. Any person, even if he is the trained and
designated representative of the law enforcement agency who is
charged with conducting lineups, but who arranged relatively few
each year, is bound to have problems in putting together a lineup

free of bias. The entire process is delicate and most vulnerable to prejudice.

In conclusion, a considerable number of psychological and legal issues that bear on eyewitness testimony have been discussed and reviewed. The author then offered his views concerning taped lineups. Succeeding chapters, much like these first three, have sought to bridge the gap between theory and practice. It is hoped that lawyers, law enforcement personnel, social scientists, students and others will have found them useful.

REFERENCES

Buckhout, R. Eyewitness Testimony. *Scientific American,* 1974, 212, 23-31.

Buckhout, R. Psychological Aspects of Eyewitness Testimony. Paper presented at the annual meeting of the New England Psychological Association, Worcester, Mass. Fall, 1977.

Buckhout, R., Figueroa, D. and Hoff, E. Eyewitness Identification: Effects of Suggestion and Bias in Identification From Photographs. *Bulletin of the Psychonomic Society,* 1975, 71-74.

Cady, H.M. On the Psychology of Testimony. American Journal of Psychology, 1924, 35, 110-112.

Freud, S. Psycho-Analysis and the Ascertaining of Truth in Courts of Law. In *Collected Papers,* (J. Riviere translation), 1953, 2, 13-24.

Gilbert v. California, 388 U.S., 263. *Supreme Court Reporter,* 1967.

Goldstein, A.V. The Fallibility of the Eyewitness: Psychological Evidence. In B. D. Sales (Ed.), *Psychology in the Legal Process.* New York: Spectrum Publications, Inc., 1977.

Goldstein, A.V. and Chance, J. Intraindividual Consistency in Visual Recognition Memory. Paper presented at American Psychological Association Convention, August 31, 1978, Toronto, Canada.

Kirby v. Illinois, 406 U.S. 682. *Supreme Court Reporter, 1971.*

LaSota, J.A. *Model Rules for Law Enforcement: Eyewitness Identification.* Tempe, Arizona: College of Law, Arizona State University and The Police Foundation, 1974.

Levine, R., Chein, I. and Murphy, G. The Learning and Forgetting of Controversial Material. *Journal of Abnormal and Social Psychology,* 1943, 38, 507-517.

Levine, F.J. and Tapp, J.L. The Psychology of Criminal Identification: The Gap from Wade to Kirby, *University of Pennsylvania Law Review,* 1973, 121, 1079-1131.

Moore v. State of Illinois, *The United States Law Week.* 46 LW 4050, December 13, 1977.

Munsterberg, H. *On the Witness Stand: Essays on Psychology and Crime.*

New York: Clark Boardman, 1908.

Neil v. Biggers, 409 U.S. 188, 193, 93 S. Ct. 375, 379, 34 L. Ed. 2nd (1972)).

Protection of the Accused at Police Lineups, Comment, *Columbia Journal of Law and Social Problems,* 1970, 6, 345-373.

Rolph, C.H. *Personal Identity.* London: Michael Joseph, 1957.

Rosenthal, R. *Experimenter Effects in Behavioral Research.* New York: Appleton-Century-Crofts, 1966.

Sobel, N.R. *Eye-Witness Identification: Legal and Practical Problems.* New York: Clark Boardman Company, Ltd., 1972.

Stern, W. The Pychology of Testimony. *Journal of Abnormal and Social Psychology,* 1939, 34, 3-20.

Stovall v. Denno, Warden, 388 U.S. 293. *Supreme Court Reporter,* 1967.

Tapp, J.L. Psychology and the Law: An Overture. In M.R. Rosenzweig and L.W. Porter (Eds.), *Annual Review of Psychology,* Volume 27, Palo Alto, California: Annual Reviews, 1976.

United States v. Ash, 413 U.S., 300. *Supreme Court Reporter,* 1973.

United States v. Wade, 388 U.S. 218. *Supreme Court Reporter,* 1967.

Uviller, R. *The Processes of Criminal Justice: Investigation and Ajudication* (Supplement). St. Paul, Minnesota: West, 1977.

Wall, P. *Eye-Witness Identification in Criminal Cases.* Springfield, Illinois: Charles C Thomas, Publisher, 1965.

Wigmore, J. *The Science of Judicial Proof.* Boston: Little, Brown & Company, 1937.

Williams, G. and Hammelman, N., Identification Parades, Part I., *Criminal Law Review,* 479-482, 1963.

Whipple, G.M. Psychology of Testimony and Report. *Psychological Bulletin,* 1912, 9, 264-269.

Whipple, G.M. The observer as Reporter: A Survey of the "Psychology of Testimony." *The Psychological Bulletin,* 1909, 6, 153-170.

Whitely, P.L. and McGeoch, J.A. The Effect of One Form of Report Upon Another. *American Journal of Psychology,* 1927, 38, 280-284.

Chapter IV

JURY DECISIONMAKING: THE U.S. SUPREME COURT

INTRODUCTION

RECENTLY, the U.S. Supreme Court, in drawing extensively on social science research findings, decided a case involving the size of juries. The case was *Ballew v. Georgia* (1978). Not only did the majority opinion cite various studies, but the entire foundation of the decision rested on these research endeavors. While many social scientists will applaud the emergence of this more receptive attitude toward the work of psychologists, sociologists and others, there is real cause for concern.

Many of the studies identified appeared to be accepted uncritically by the Court. A brief dissenting note, in the context of his concurring opinion, was offered by Justice Powell *(Ballew v. Georgia,* 1978) when he opined, "Also, I have reservations as to the wisdom as well as the necessity of Mr. Justice Blackmun's heavy reliance on numerology derived from statistical studies. Moreover, neither the validity nor the methodology employed by the studies cited was subjected to the traditional testing mechanisms of the adversary process" (p. 4224).

While the many studies cited by the majority do have a face validity that is very inviting, some of them have a variety of problems associated with the methods and subjects employed.

Buckhout (1977), among others, shared this author's concern regarding the Court's interpretation of social science research findings in the *Williams v. Florida* (1969) case when he stated, "The Court's reference to the convincing nature of the empirical evidence reviewed is especially disturbing. Three of the four

117

studies noted were archival analyses, examining selected civil cases tried by six– and twelve-member juries, in selected jurisdictions. With such references, the Court stretches the social scientists' concept of what constitutes 'empirical evidence'" (p. 22) .

Historically, the responses of the judiciary to social science research findings suggest a "pendulum" type of effect. Earlier in history, as this author has already pointed out, there were instances in which the legal community turned a deaf ear to the reports of psychologists, sociologists, and other behavioral scientists, but more recently the Court appears to have uncritically accepted research findings.

Justice Powell's *(Ballew,* 1978) caution about relying on "numerology" in his concurring opinion appears to have been the most significant critical statement concerning wholesale acceptance of the research studies, but his comment was very general. In *Williams v. Florida* (1970) and somewhat later in *Colgrove v. Battin* (1973), the Supreme Court was even less critical in its general acceptance of research that was related to the problem. As Goldstein (1978) recently commented in his report on *Ballew* (1978). "Once before the Court was apparently stung by its reliance on empirical jury studies" (p. Al) . The Court clearly erred in its reliance upon a handful of unsound empirical studies. In *Ballew* (1978), however, reference to Saks' (1977) work indicated that the Court was exposed to the major criticisms that had been voiced earlier.

The fundamental problem of extending laboratory findings to the "real world" is raised. Some of the studies to be reviewed in the next chapter, including some of those cited by the U.S. Supreme Court in *Ballew* are "simulations" and social-psychological experiments undertaken with students as subjects. These studies, which have sought to replicate "real life" jury processes, undoubtedly have much to offer the courts, but judges and the experts available to them need to examine all such data with a jaundiced eye. The behavior of real-life jurors, experiencing an undercurrent of tension and pressure in making a decision about a man's life (as they are sometimes required to do) , may be quite different from the mock jury behavior that social psychologists enthusiastically observe.

The *Ballew v. Georgia* (1978) decision involved the Supreme Court's statement concerning five-man juries. Many of the studies undertaken since *Williams v. Florida* in 1969 have examined the effect of size on outcome and process. In that earlier opinion, the Court held that the constitutional guarantee of a trial by jury does not require that jury membership be fixed at twelve, and they refused to disturb Florida's law concerning the use of six-man juries. The Court's latest statement on the problem of size offered the view that a five-man jury was unacceptable and a line had to be drawn somewhere. The details of the Supreme Court's views in this area will be elaborated on at a later point.

Understandably, psychologists have been eager to investigate the jury process in light of the Supreme Court's expressed interest in the matter. Group dynamics, a sub-field within social psychology, offers an excellent frame of reference for those scholars interested in unraveling jury decisionmaking processes. The way in which people generally go about making decisions has also been of interest to social psychologists as evidenced by a current work by Janis and Mann (1978). Asch's (1973) classic work on group conformity also helps to shed light on group decision making. As many writers have pointed out, however, the frustration associated with jury research is directly linked to the problem of obtaining access to real-life juries. Law now prohibits the observation, taping, recording, etc. of real life jury deliberations and therefore social scientists have relied on "mock ups" in their attempts to elucidate the processes involved.

Another natural avenue of pursuit has to do with the study of the psychological characteristics of defendants, witnesses and jurors. Their impact on jury deliberations and decisions is obviously important. It is quite evident that the personality characteristics of the "actors" influence the outcome of trials. While ideally the issues of the case should determine the outcome, the sympathies elicited by defendants, for example, appear to significantly affect the observations of juries and judges. This issue was illuminated in the discrepancies found between judges and juries in Kalven and Zeisel's (1970) classic work entitled *The American Jury*. In that study, defendants appeared to be more frequently successful in eliciting the sympathy of jurors than judges, with subsequent verdicts being affected.

The question of the importance of defendant attractiveness will be examined in the context of similarities between jurors and defendants. The psychological role of *identification,* as defined by psychoanalytical writers, is helpful in this respect. Perceiving a likeness with another, at an unconscious level, will affect our attitude toward him or her. To the extent that he or she seems to be "one of us," we are apt to be sympathetic to his or her plight.

The use of videotape in the courtroom has created a wave of interest on the part of the judiciary, and social scientists have eagerly jumped in to examine its impact. A number of symposia, studies, and commentary have been offered by scholars, and this literature will be reviewed. Not unlike the problem of simulating jury deliberations, the question of the validity of videotaping witnesses, crime scenes, and entire trials is raised. What is their impact on judge and jury? Does videotaping present a significantly different stimulus for the decision-maker to react to the outcome; does it vary from what one might expect if the "real thing" were observed?

And then there is the question of pretrial publicity. It appears that this question is constantly raised as the "free press" vigorously attempts to uncover stories, investigate wrongdoing, and shed light on crime and conviction. But what about the rights of defendants to a fair trial? A series of cases in recent years, described extensively by others, provide evidence of this on-going battle between the press and the judiciary. These and other issues related to jury decision-making will be discussed and analyzed in this and subsequent chapters.

United States Supreme Court Decisions

The U.S. Constitution guarantee of a trial by jury does not require that the jury number *twelve.* The case of *Williams v. Florida* (1970) offered the U. S. Supreme Court an opportunity to present their views on this matter of size and they seized it. Florida's rule concerning "notice-of-alibi" was also ruled on by the Court.

The petitioner was tried for robbery in the State of Florida.

Prior to his trial, he filed a motion to impanel a twelve-man jury required by Florida law. This motion was denied at the trial level and the District Court of Appeals affirmed, rejecting the petitioner's claims that his Sixth Amendment rights had been violated. The Supreme Court granted certiorari.

In the case of *Duncan v. Louisiana* (1968), the Court had held that the Fourteenth Amendment guarantees a right to trial by jury in all criminal cases that, if tried in court, would come within the Sixth Amendment's guarantee. They went on to point out that "providing an accused with the right to be tried by a jury of his peers gave him an inestimable safeguard against the corrupt or overzealous prosecutor and against the compliant, biased, or eccentric judge" (p. 100).

The Court phrased the issue raised by *Williams* (1970) as follows: "The question in this case then is whether the Constitutional guarantee of a trial by 'jury' necessarily requires trial by exactly twelve persons, rather than some lesser number, in this case six. We hold that the six-man panel is not a necessary ingredient of 'trial by jury,' and that respondent's refusal to impanel more than the six members provided by Florida law did not violate petitioner's Sixth Amendment rights as applied to the States through the Fourteenth" (p. 86).

The Court's opinion in *Williams* (1970) reviewed briefly the history of jury trials in Europe, as well as America, seeking a rationale that would either support or reject the concept of the twelve-man jury. Noting that there was a long tradition of relying on a body of one's peers to determine guilt or innocence (as a protection against the arbitrary use of authority by law enforcement), they found the question of number obscure.

During the days of the Frankish empire and the so-called "inquisition," there was no fixed number and the numbers varied from sixty-six, forty-one, twenty, seventeen, thirteen, eleven, eight, seven, fifty-three and fifteen, according to James Thayer in his *The Jury and Its Development* (1892).

In general, it appears that somewhere around the time of the fourteenth century, the size of the jury became fixed at twelve, but as the Court suggests, it appears to have been a historical accident.

While earlier decisions of the U.S. Supreme Court have affirmed the use of twelve (see *Thompson v. Utah* [1898]) , none has confronted the question head on. After reviewing some of the language of the U. S. Constitution, the Court in *Williams* (1969) stated:

> It may be that the usual expectation was that the jury would consist of 12, and that hence, the most likely conclusion to be drawn is simply that little thought was actually given to the specific question we face today. But there is absolutely no indication in "the intent of the framers" of an explicit decision to equate the constitutional and common-law characteristics of the jury. Nothing in this history suggests, then, that we do violence to the letter of the Constitution by turning to other than purely historical considerations to determine which features of the jury system, as it existed at common law, were preserved in the Constitution. The relevant inquiry, as we see it, must be the function that the particular feature performs and its relation to the purposes of the jury trial. Measured by this standard, the 12 man requirement cannot be regarded as an indispensable component of the Sixth Amendment. (p. 99)

The Court went on to point out that a primary feature of a jury trial involved the "interposition" between the accused and accuser of the commonsense judgment of a group of laymen, and in the "community participation and shared responsibility" that emerged from the group's deliberations. Also offered was the observation that the group should be large enough to obtain a "representative cross-section of the community" but that this could be achieved with a jury of six members as well as twelve. Finally, in linking the unanimity requirement to size, the Court offered the view that the process of deliberation was safeguarded against. *While citing a number of scholarly articles to support its position, most of those materials were opinions offered by legal scholars rather than scientific research findings which were yet to emerge.*

In referring to the number of varied viewpoints brought to bear in twelve vs. six-man juries, the Court ventured a position which has received no support in subsequent studies of jury behavior. They suggested that *(Williams v. Florida,* 1970) ; "Similarly, while in theory the number of viewpoints represented on a randomly selected jury ought to increase as the size of the jury increases, in practice the difference between the 12-man and the 6-man jury in terms of the cross-section of the community represented seems likely to be negligible. Even the 12-man jury cannot insure representation of every distinct voice in the community, particularly given the use of the peremptory challenge" (p. 102) .

Dissenting opinions, offered by among others Justices Marshall and Harlan, added little to the debate except that they stressed the importance of the historical precedent of twelve. In effect, Justice Marshall asked, "What new evidence has emerged that we should alter the traditional reliance on twelve?" Justice Harlan pointed out that the number six was as arbitrary as twelve.

In *Johnson v. Louisiana* (1972) and in *Apodaca v. Oregon* (1972) the U. S. Supreme Court tackled different but related issues. Johnson had been convicted of a robbery by a nine to three verdict upon trial in the Criminal District Court of the Parish of New Orleans. Later, the Louisiana Court affirmed the conviction, rejecting the defendant's position that "the due process clause of the Fourteenth Amendment was violated by the provisions for conviction by less than a unanimous verdict, and that such provisions were also invalid under the equal protection clause since under Louisiana law, unanimity was required in twelve-man jury capital cases and in five-man jury cases in which punishment at hard labor might be imposed" (p. 152) .

The U. S. Supreme Court noted at the outset of its opinion that it had never held that jury unanimity was a requirement of due process of law. The majority opinion stated that it was their view that the petitioner's argument broke down into two parts. First, that nine jurors would be unable to vote conscientiously in favor of guilt beyond a reasonable doubt when three of their colleagues argued for acquittal. Second, that guilt could not be said to have been proven beyond a reasonable doubt when one or more of a jury's members at the end of deliberation still possessed a doubt.

The Court rejected both arguments. In the first instance, they pointed out that merely because three jurors dissented did not in and of itself suggest that the nine others were not conscientious in deliberating and reaching a conclusion. In addition, they noted that the opposite would probably be true, namely:

A juror presenting reasoned argument in favor of acquittal would either have his arguments answered or would carry enough other jurors with him to prevent conviction. A majority will cease discussion and outvote a minority only after reasoned discussion has ceased to have persuasive affect or to serve any other purpose—when a minority, that is, continues to insist upon acquittal without having persuasive reasons in support of its position. At that juncture there is no basis for denigrating the vote of so large a majority of the jury or for refusing to accept their decision as being, at least in their minds, beyond a reasonable doubt. Indeed, at this point, a "dissenting juror should consider whether his doubt was a reasonable one—[when it made no impression upon the minds of so many men, equally honest, equally intelligent with himself]." (p. 159)

Concerning the second argument, the U. S. Supreme Court observed that jury verdicts finding guilt beyond a reasonable doubt are regularly sustained even though the evidence might have justified a reasonable doubt and that a trial judge might not have reached a similar conclusion. One of the major findings, of course, from *The American Jury* (1971) project was that judges and juries frequently differed on verdicts. As part of the position advanced in this majority opinion, the justices referred to the jury process in federal court. In that instance, they noted that juries operating under a unanimity rule are instructed to acquit a defendant if they have a reasonable doubt about his guilt. In addition, they indicated that if the doubt of a minority of jurors suggested the existence of a reasonable doubt, it would appear that a defendant should receive a directed verdict rather than a retrial. Finally, concerning the Louisiana Legislature's adoption of a law requiring unanimous verdicts in capital cases vs. less than unanimous verdicts in other cases, the Court stated that they saw nothing unconstitutional about this law.

Acknowledging that Louisiana made conviction more difficult in capital cases by requiring the assent of all twelve (as compared with less than unanimous verdicts in other cases) this nonetheless did not constitute a denial of equal protection of the law. They stated simply that "The State may treat capital offenders differently without violating the constitutional rights of those charged with lesser crimes" (p. 161).

Much of the discussion offered in majority as well as dissenting opinions concerning the unanimity issue also applied to *Apodaca v. Oregon* (1972) which was decided on the same day and dealt with the same general problem.   In that case, Oregon law authorized verdicts by ten of twelve jurors in criminal cases, except for first degree murder verdicts.   Three defendants were convicted in separate trials, for non-first degree murder offenses, by eleven-to-one (two cases), and ten-to-two verdicts.   Justice White's majority opinion initially referred to historical precedent.   He traced the unanimity requirement back to the Middle Ages, and noted that it was an accepted part of the common law jury in the eighteenth century, but he then went on to raise the question of *function,* as the Court had done earlier in *Williams.*   In this context he stated:

> A requirement of unanimity, however, does not materially contribute to the exercise of this commonsense judgment.   As we said in Williams, a jury will come to such a judgment as long as it consists of a group of laymen representative of a cross-section of the community who have the duty and the opportunity to deliberate free from outside attempts at intimidation, on the question of a defendant's guilt.   In terms of this function we perceive no difference between juries required to act unanimously and those permitted to convict or acquit by votes of 10 to two or 11 to one." (p. 191)

Justice Powell's concurring opinion which spoke to the parallel issues raised by both *Apodaca* and *Johnson* and referring to the relationship of the federal system to that of the states, noted that the Fourteenth Amendment did not require "blind adherence" by the states to all details of the federal Sixth Amendment standards.   He went on to observe that he did not believe that the Civil War Amendments were intended to deprive the states of all freedom to experiment with variations in jury trials.   It is at this point that the idea of a "laboratory" and "empirical" approach is interjected into the discussion:

> In an age in which empirical study is increasingly relied upon as a foundation for decision making, one of the more obvious merits of our federal system is the opportunity it affords each state, if its people so choose, to become a "laboratory" and to experiment with a range of trial and procedural alternatives.   Although the need for the innovations that grow out of diversity has always been great, imagination unimpeded by unwarranted demands for material uniformity is

of special importance at a time when serious doubt exists as to the adequacy of our criminal justice system. (p. 167)

Citing a number of scholarly legal opinions and Kalven and Zeisel (1971), he goes on to buttress his position by noting that the removal of the unanimity requirement could well minimize the potential for hung juries "occasioned either by bribery or juror irrationality." In a specific reference to *The American Jury,* he offers, "Furthermore, the rule that juries must speak with a single voice often leads, not to full agreement among the twelve but to agreement by none and compromise by all, despite the frequent absence of a rational basis for such compromise (p. 168).

In presenting a vigorous dissent, Justice Douglas advanced the idea that debate will be reduced under non-unanimous verdicts. This issue was to come under study later in psychological experimental simulations of the jury process. At that point in time, Douglas offered a view from his own base of experience: "It is said that there is no evidence that majority jurors will refuse to listen to dissenters whose votes are unneeded for conviction. Yet human experience teaches that polite and academic conversation is no substitute for the earnest and robust argument necessary to reach unanimity" (p. 169).

In reviewing the Supreme Court opinions in *Williams, Johnson,* and *Apodaca,* it is evident that the Court was becoming more receptive to empirical research evidence but had very little research evidence available to it with the exception of *The American Jury.* It was at this point that social scientists, and psychologists in particular, saw an opening and began to generate studies.

The issue of jury size once again came before the Court in *Colgrove v. Battin* (1973). In this instance, the focus was the question of size as it related to the federal court system. The case concerned a civil suit in which the petitioner argued that under the Seventh Amendment and 28 U.S.C. 2072, he was entitled to trial by twelve persons. However, Local Rule 13 (d)(1) of the Revised Rules of Procedure of the United States District Court for the District of Montana provided that a jury for trial of civil matters should consist of six persons.

Justice Brennan's majority opinion noted that in *Williams v. Florida* (1970), the Court had left open the question of whether "additional references to the 'common law' that occur in the Seventh Amendment might support a different interpretation" in the context of civil cases. The Court decided that they did not. They stated: "Constitutional history reveals no intention on the part of the framers 'to equate the common law characteristics of the jury' " (p. 156). Much of the opinion went over ground already broken in *Williams* (1970). At one point, the justices stated that while a number of studies had been undertaken since *Williams* (1970), they saw "nothing that persuades us to depart from the conclusion reached in *Williams*."

While they were later to regret their endorsement of *four very recent studies which provided convincing empirical evidence* of the correctness of the *Williams* conclusion, the efforts of social science researchers were beginning to be heard with greater regularity. Thus, the Court concluded that a jury of six satisfied the Seventh Amendment's guarantee of trial by jury in civil cases.

The "four recent studies" were later to be criticized severely by Saks (1977), Zeisel and Diamond (1974) and others. Saks' (1977) criticism was later noted in the *Ballew v. Georgia* (1978) decision when the Court decided to hold the line at six jurors. They will be discussed in the next chapter.

While some members of the Court were demonstrating an increased interest in empirical studies, not all of the justices were persuaded of their value. Justice Marshall, in a dissenting opinion, offered his criticism by stating, "The Court today elects to abandon the certainty of this historical test, as well as the many cases which support it, in favor of a vaguely defined functional analysis which asks not what the framers mean by 'trial by jury' but rather whether some substitute for the common-law jury performs the same functions as a jury and serves as an adequate substitute for one" (p. 179).

The hostility that Marshall felt for the decision is reflected in this statement:

> I think history will bear out the proposition that when constitutional rights are grounded in nothing more solid than the intuitive, unexplained sense of five Justices that a certain line is "right" or just, those rights are certain to erode and, eventually, disappear altogether. Today, a majority of this Court may find six-man juries to represent a

proper balance between competing demands of expedition and group representation. But as dockets become more crowded and pressures on jury trials grow, who is to say that some future Court will not find three, or two, or one a number large enough to satisfy its unexplicated sense of justice. (p. 181)

In completing the survey of the most noteworthy U. S. Supreme Court decisions on the jury process, we return to the most recent case of *Ballew v. Georgia* (1978). As the reader may recall, the Court decided that based on a number of research studies, a five-man jury was unacceptable. In this case, the Court held that the five-member jury does not satisfy the jury trial guarantee of the Sixth Amendment, as applied to the states through the Fourteenth. They went on to indicate that neither the financial benefit nor the time-saving benefit, which were both claimed by Georgia, were significant enough to offset the constitutional guarantees that reducing the jury from six to five would afford.

The author will return to some of the main issues identified in the *Ballew* decision after the research studies which undergirded it have been reviewed and analyzed. The following chapter reports on much of the scientific work cited by the Court in its *Ballew* decision.

REFERENCES

Apodaca v. Oregon 32 L Ed 2d, *U.S. Supreme Court Reports,* 1972.

Asch, S. Studies of Independence and Conformity: A Minority of One Against A Unanimous Majority, *Psychological Review,* 1973, 80, 97-125.

Ballew v. Georgia, 1978, 46 *U.S.L.W.* 4217.

Buckhout, R. The U.S. Supreme Court vs. Social Science: The Jury, Unpublished Manuscript (CR-28), Center for Responsive Psychology, Brooklyn College, 1977.

Colgrove v. Battin, 413 U.S. 149, *U.S. Supreme Court Reports,* 1973.

Duncan v. Louisiana, 391 U.S. 145, *U.S. Supreme Court Reports,* 1968.

Goldstein, T. Defendant Seen At Disadvantage in U.S. Trend to Smaller Juries, *New York Times,* April 25, 1978, A1.

Janis, I. and Mann, L. *Decisionmaking,* Free Press, 1977.

Johnson v. Louisiana 32 L Ed. 2d, *U.S. Supreme Court Reports,* 1972.

Kalven, H. and Zeisel, H. *The American Jury.* Chicago: The University of Chicago Press (Phoenix Edition), 1971.

Saks, M.   *Jury Verdicts.*   Lexington, Massachusetts: Lexington Books, 1977.

Thayer, J.B.   The Jury and Its Development.   *Harvard Law Review,* 1892, 5,295.

Thompson v. Utah, 170 U.S. 343.   *U.S. Supreme Court Reports,* 1898.

Williams v. Florida, 399 U.S. 78, *U.S. Supreme Court Reports,* 1970.

Zeisel, H. and Diamond, S.   Convincing Empirical Evidence of the Six Member Jury.   *University of Chicago Law Review,* 1974, 41, 281-295.

Chapter V

JURY DECISIONMAKING:
ISSUES OF SIZES AND UNANIMITY

THE JURY SYSTEM has a very long history that dates back to the Middle Ages, as noted in the previous chapter. Support for it rests on two assumptions according to Nemeth (1976) :

> On the one hand the jury system tends to allay fears of political entanglements. On the other hand proponents of the system emphasize that the decision of twelve is better than the decision of one, even if professional experience is lacking. And some even acclaim the importance of the lack of professional experience. The lay jury has a fresh perception of each trial and the introduction of common sense and common experience is considered to be a valuable asset. (p. 169)

Others have cited the value of community participation in the process. Kalven and Zeisel (1971) have pointed out that because of its transient nature, the jury acts as a type of "lightning rod" with respect to hostility and emotional reaction which is not infrequently aroused by trials. This displacement of emotion on to the jury relieves the judge of this burden. In the political realm, there are many who believe that the jury is less vulnerable to corruption than a single judge would be—once again because of the transient character of the jury versus the more permanent quality of the judicial appointee. Also, a jury of six or twelve persons compared to the single judge presents a more formidable barrier to a potential corrupter.

While jurisdictions vary concerning the practice of plea bargaining, it is so widespread throughout America that even after the prosecutor has decided to move forward, only a very small percentage of cases come to trial. Approximately 14 percent of all felony prosecutions end in jury trials, according to Kalven and Zeisel (1971).

As previously noted, much of the research concerning size and unanimity emerged after the *Williams v. Florida* (1970) case. Jurists had little empirical evidence to guide them as they sought to unravel the mysteries of jury deliberations. However, Kalven and Zeisel's (1971) classic work was available at that time, but as any number of scholars have pointed out, the data it furnished were not always interpreted accurately by the Courts.

The University of Chicago jury project was spearheaded by a social scientist and a lawyer. Beyond the main finding, that judges and juries frequently differ in their judgments concerning trials, with juries more often siding with defendants, other significant information regarding jury behavior emerged.

The researchers obtained reports on 3,576 trials. While these were not selected on a random basis, the authors make a reasonably good case for the representativeness of the data they obtained.

Questionnaires were developed and sent to 555 judges who agreed to participate. They were asked, basically, to describe how the jury decided a case and how they would have decided a case for those conducted before them. A major finding of the study was the fact that the judge and jury agreed in 75.4 percent of all the trials included in the sample. This included agreement to acquit in 13.4 percent of the cases and agreement to convict in 62.0 percent of the cases. Regarding the disagreement (24.6 percent of all cases) between judge and jury, they divided in 19.1 percent of the cases over guilt and 5.5 percent of the time when the jury hung. In examining the direction of the disagreement, the defendant fared better 16 percent of the time when he was given the option of a jury trial over a bench trial. As the researchers noted, however, the 16 percent figure may be misleading because the cases to which this figure applied had been selected for jury trial because the defense had anticipated pro defendant sympathy.

STUDIES OF JURY DECISIONMAKING

Bermant and Coppock (1973) studied Workmen's Compensation Act cases in an effort to shed light on six– versus twelve-person juries. These civil cases allowed for either jury or bench trials, and jury size may be less than twelve, if both sides agree. The trial involves the reading of the transcript of the formal administrative hearing with the lawyers playing all the roles in the reading. For 1970, 128 jury trials of this type were conducted in the state of Washington, including ninety-five trials of twelve-person juries and thirty-three of six-person juries. The outcomes were very similar in terms of verdicts for the plaintiffs versus those for the Department of Labor and Industries. The authors concluded that:

> If we may properly assume that the assignment of jury size was essentially random in respect to the merits of the cases under consideration, then we may conclude that the use of the smaller jury introduced no systematic bias into the trial outcomes. Hence, given the additional advantages of the smaller jury, its increased use is recommended. (p. 595)

As a number of critics have pointed out [including Saks (1975), Kessler (1975), and Zeisel and Diamond (1975)] there were serious weaknesses in the research. Zeisel and Diamond (1974) pointed to the fact that the attorneys had the option of demanding the larger-sized jury and that they seemingly exercised it for the larger, more involved cases. They noted that the fee for a twelve-member jury is usually twice that for a six-member jury. Saks (1977) presented his criticism regarding the Bermant and Coppock (1973) statement on randomization in the following manner: "That assumption may, however, not be justified. All correlational studies, in contrast to experiments, admit the possibility that some third, unmeasured variable confounded the results, and that a difference or lack of one is caused not by the relationship between the variables of interest but by that third variable" (p. 39). He went on to say that in the Washington study, attorneys may have consistently chosen the size of the jury based on the characteristics of the case and, therefore, the basis of comparison between six and twelve-member juries was destroyed.

Another study which employed a correlational technique was that undertaken by the Institute of Judicial Administration in 1972. The 650 civil cases reviewed were from the state of New Jersey, and like the previously mentioned study, the litigants were given a choice of jury size. These scholars also found no differences in verdicts (58.0 percent for the plaintiffs in six-member jury trials; 57.3 percent for the plaintiffs in twelve-member jury trials). It likewise was criticized for the same reason that the Bermant and Coppock (1973) design was attacked—a built-in bias favored one size jury over another, depending on the issues involved. Saks (1977) pointed to the fact that twelve-member juries considered cases in which approximately triple the amount of damages were at issue substantiated this contention. Concerning the length of trials and deliberation time, he (Saks, 1977) added, "This difference in trial time and the parallel difference in deliberation time (longer for cases going to twelve-person juries) are consistent with the hypothesis that the cases tried to twelve-member juries were more complex than those tried to six-member juries" (p. 42).

In a study undertaken by Mills (1973), he attempted to shed light on the question of six– versus twelve-person juries. In this instance, the comparison was drawn between two different-sized juries operating in the same court system for different time periods. The investigator pointed to two limitations which were later expanded upon by critics—the different-sized juries deliberated different cases and "other changes besides the jury size modification may have occurred between or during the two time periods under consideration" (p. 675). Zeisel and Diamond (1974) later identified "other changes" which may have affected the outcome. They mentioned that a mediation board was instituted, and procedural rules were modified to allow discovery of insurance policy limits. Nonetheless, the study found "no statistically significant differences between six-member and twelve-member jury verdicts in civil cases in Wayne County Circuit Court.

A confusing aspect involved the size of the awards offered by the juries in these civil cases. The smaller panels appeared to have issued greater damage awards, but the researcher (attempting to adjust for inflation) reduced the awards downward for the juries which functioned after July 23, 1970. Michigan state law mandated six-member juries after the above-mentioned data. However, the role of the mediation board and settlements which emerged in response to the discovery of insurance limits may have affected the amounts in question (Zeisel and Diamond, 1974).

Kessler (1973) sought to answer the question, is the *deliberative process* different for six vs. twelve-person jury panels? Her study, like the others identified by the Supreme Court's majority in *Colgrove v. Battin* (1973), was one of the now infamous "four recent studies" which provided "convincing empirical evidence" of the lack of significant differences between six vs. twelve-person juries. She employed a videotaped dramatization of an actual automobile negligence case which had been settled out of court. This videotaped trial was presented to eight juries of six persons and eight juries of twelve persons. Jurors were 144 undergraduate students enrolled in speech classes at the University of Michigan. The researcher attempted to support her use of college student subjects by citing another scholar's (Forston, 1968) doctoral dissertation which apparently found little difference between real jurors and college students. Critics have cited the type of subjects employed in jury research as critical to the deliberative process as well as to the outcome.

After viewing the trial, the mock juries privately recorded their verdicts and then each jury deliberated on a verdict. While the study found no significant differences (statistically) between verdicts of six and twelve-person juries, the nature of the case (extremely onesided) and the relatively small sample size of jury panels appears to have invalidated the results (Zeiseland Diamond, 1974; Saks, 1977).

Other criticisms also emerged. The fact that the mock juries were instructed according to Michigan law, in which agreement of five out of six, or ten out of twelve constitutes a verdict, created a problem because the data revealed that prior to deliberating, many of the juries had reached the required majority. Thus, only six juries out of twelve engaged in "meaningful deliberations" (Zeisel and Diamond, 1974).

The fact that six-person juries did not differ from twelve-person juries on the variable of deliberation time was also questioned by Diamond (1974) in her reanalysis of Kessler's (1973) original experiment. Given the one-sided nature of the trial, combined with the small number of jury panels, it was pointed out that this finding was meaningless. The use of a videotaped trial, while preferable to some other simulation techniques employed by other researchers, may have further affected the group process and outcome of the jury panels in some unknown way. Data concerning the use of videotaped trials in real trials will be discussed in a later chapter.

Also widely cited as a piece of research which focused on jury behavior is the work of Valenti and Downing (1975). They randomly assigned 360 male and female students enrolled in political science classes at the University of Georgia to six– and twelve-member juries. The juries were further divided into those which were exposed to evidence slightly weighted in favor of acquittal (low apparent guilt) and those exposed to evidence which slightly favored conviction (high apparent guilt). Concerning the pre-deliberation status of jurors, a check of guilty vs. not guilty notes on the first ballot indicated that the apparent guilt manipulation had been effective and no statistically significant differences between jurors emerged as a function of size. These researchers claimed to have found, however, differences between six and twelve-member juries when high apparent guilt was suggested. Specifically, guilty verdicts emerged in nine out of ten six-member juries, while only two out of ten twelve-member juries returned guilty verdicts for this condition. No significant differences were found for the different-sized jury panels for the low apparent guilt condition. Thus, it would appear that the twelve-member panel safeguards the rights of defendants to a greater degree than its smaller counterpart.

Criticisms of this study have to include the problem of employing students as subjects. They have relatively little invested in the process and regardless of how successful the experiments are in motivating them, it is difficult to imagine that they behaved in ways consistent with those of a cross-section of adults in a given jurisdiction. In addition to being younger on the average than a representative group of jurors, it is highly probable that they were more liberal than their real-life counterparts.

Once again, sample size remained relatively small, particularly after subjects were split into high and low guilt conditions. Saks (1977) uncovered methodological flaws in this study and in a re-analysis of the data reported that the apparent significant differences on the "high guilt" condition vanished. He pointed to the fact that pretreatment differences had existed and that they paralleled the posttreatment differences, thus leaving the question open as to what factor had been responsible for the observed outcome found by Valenti and Downing (1975).

Davis, Kerr, Atkins, Holt, and Meek (1975) assigned six– and twelve-member juries to both unanimous and two-thirds majority rule conditions. Like others, they drew on college students for subjects. All mock jurors listened to a simulated rape case, deliberated, and then offered verdicts consistent with the rule conditions assigned. Neither assigned rule nor jury size had an effect upon verdicts. Saks (1977) cited a recurring problem: because the trial was heavily biased, no one jury in any condition arrived at a guilty verdict. Thus, the severely biased trial, according to Saks, so distorts the results that they are rendered uninterpretable.

Earlier, Lampert's (1975) criticism of "real world" jury research appeared to be in the same vein—"most cases will so clearly favor one party that studies of actual trials are unlikely to reveal substantial differences in the percentage of plaintiff or prosecution verdicts rendered by different-sized juries" (p. 699).

Padawer-Singer, Singer, and Singer (1977) conducted jury research which they felt was sensitive to many of the previously identified criticisms. They touted the fact that they obtained real jurors who had come from the central jury room of an authentic court (in cooperation with Queens County Supreme Court Judge Charles Margett). A videotaped reenactment of an actual trial was presented to the participants. Also, as in real trials, the jurors were allowed as much time to deliberate as they required (two or three days, if necessary). Their main focus was on the effect of six vs. twelve-member panels and unanimous vs. non-unanimous rules. The sample was somewhat larger than those reported by other researchers; twenty-three juries existed for each of the four categories when size interacts with decision rule (unanimous vs. non-unanimous).

In reporting their findings, Padawer-Singer et al. (1977) point out that the Supreme Court's assumption that six-member juries will deliberate thoroughly is not borne out. They note, "There appears to be an element of greater 'instability' in six-member juries; chance factors and curtailed deliberations seem to determine the verdicts in almost one of four six-member juries, while this is not the case in twelve-member juries" (p. 82). Hung juries occurred in all types except from among the six-member non-unanimous types. Interestingly, the authors found no significant differences in verdicts on either the variable of size or decision rule. The authors caution the reader that this last finding may be due to the particular case (shades of Saks' (1977) earlier criticism concerning the lack of variability in the dependent variable), the small number of juries tested, or that differences may exist but not in directionality. Finally, hung juries occurred with equal frequency in twelve-member unanimous, twelve-member non-unanimous, and six-member unanimous juries.

In contrast to the Padawer-Singer et al. (1977) findings, a group at the Center For Responsive Psychology (Buckhout, Weg, Reilly, and Frohboese, 1977) found differences between mock juries of six vs. twelve and those functioning under majority vs. unanimous rules. They included 180 "real life" jurors from the jury assembly in the Kings County, New York Supreme Court, who viewed a mock trial presented on videotape. For jury size, the investigators found that six-person panels tended to return more severe verdicts while twelve-person panels presented less severe verdicts. The number of convictions, however, was the same. Regarding the decision rule, in the case of a unanimous verdict, the most likely outcome was a hung jury, but the majority rule (5/6 or 10/12) proved advantageous to the prosecution side.

Grofman's (1976) work on jury decisionmaking processes resulted in his statement of a number of propositions. He relied on data generated from a number of studies already discussed in this section and he further relied on "probability theory and combinatorial mathematics" as devices for his analysis. He emerged with the following propositions:

—The effect of the group conformity process that appears to operate in juries is to exaggerate the initial majority sentiment in the direction of a unanimous verdict consonant with the views of the initial majority.
—When juries are allowed to reach non-unanimous verdicts, the probability that the jurors will have already achieved sufficient consensus for a verdict before they begin deliberation is extremely

high in small-sized juries.

—[It should be remembered that for one] who is looking for differences between six– and twelve-member juries that the nature of those differences will depend upon the extent of predeliberation accord as to verdict among the pool from which jurors are drawn.

—Because of the group conformity process that has been observed to operate in jury decisionmaking, it is very likely that shifts from unanimous to non-unanimous verdicts will have minimal impact on verdict outcomes as long as jury size is held constant. It appears to be the case that juries that began as near unanimous end up unanimous with virtual certainty. Thus, we would expect a change from a unanimity to a nonunanimity rule to have zero impact, except perhaps as to deliberation time. (p. 162-165).

Two companion studies which focused on the decision rule were reported by Nemeth (1975). In the first study, undergraduate students at the University of Virginia served as subjects while for the second study, eighty-four subjects (twelve volunteers each) observed seven different mock trials as part of a trial court practice course offered to third-year law students. Nemeth (1975) reports that findings from both studies were very similar. From a statistical standpoint, there were no significant differences in verdicts reached between groups functioning with a unanimous rule vs. those who functioned under a two-thirds majority rule. Unanimity groups did tend to be hung more often. The deliberation process appeared to have been clearly affected, as few groups under a majority mandate deliberated until consensus was achieved. The author also reports that under a majority rule, the debate lacked the *robustness* that Justice Douglas had been concerned about in conjunction with his minority opinion offered in *Johnson v. Louisiana* (1972) and *Apodaca v. Oregon* (1972).

Concerning the lack of differences (statistical) finding, the reader is now all too familiar with the problem of small sample sizes. The groups did not agree on all verdicts and it is possible that with a much larger sample, the outcome might have easily differed. Similar to criticisms voiced in regard to other studies, the presentations may have lacked realism in both cases, particularly in the first study in which the college students were exposed to a criminal case "presented in written form." While mock trials that are played out for the benefit of assisting law students in their preparation to be trial lawyers—as in the second study—may offer some of the real life drama that a good play provides, a criminal case "presented in written form" would appear to be far inferior. One could reasonably ask, is it possible to capture any of the flavor of a real-life courtroom drama by using such an approach?

Once again there is the problem of using college students as subjects (at least in the first study) but an even greater problem for this study—along with a number of the others described in this section—is involved with the deliberation process itself. *Is it possible for any group of research subjects pretending to be jurors to experience both the trial stimulus and subsequent jury deliberations in a manner that even approaches what real-life jurors experience? This issue goes to the heart of the question of the validity of experimental work in this area.* In some ways it is a question that is unanswerable, at least in precise terms, because research on real life jury deliberations is not possible, and therefore laboratory experimetnal work cannot be cross-checked against it.

After reviewing many of the major studies on jury decision-making, the author has determined that Saks' (1977) work is among the best to date. While not free of limitations—any study can be criticized on some level—he appears to have dealt rather well with some of the problems of earlier scientific investigations. Only the Padawer-Singer et al. (1977) research rivals Saks' work for overall quality. His critical findings emerged from his second experiment with former jurors from the Franklin County region of Ohio. His first experiment, which closely paralleled his second, relied on college students, but its main purpose of serving as a kind of "shakedown cruise" or pilot study appears to have been profitable.

The study would have been noteworthy for its thoroughness and comprehensiveness if for nothing else, but it did offer much more. He collected extensive data on the subjects' observations, reactions to each other (sociometric), responses during deliberations, feelings of confidence in verdicts rendered, performances in six-person panels vs. twelve-person panels, behavior under unanimous and nonunanimous decision rules, etc. While his pilot study (referred to as Experiment #1) used a written transcript of a trial adapted from a law school text, the main study (Experiment #2) offered a videotape of a staged trial in which the actors were chosen carefully for their professional knowledge of the roles. Saks (1977) pointed to the fact that since a number of subjects inquired as to whether the trial was real, this was evidence for the notion that it was an effective stimulus. At the termination of the trial presentation, jurors were asked to indicate on a questionnaire as to how certain they were of guilt or innocence. Jury deliberations were monitored through a one-way window. Two hundred sixty-four undergraduates at Ohio State University comprised the sample of experiment #1, while 461 former jurors were organized into fifty-eight juries in Experimenter #2. A small financial reward of $5.00 was offered to each former juror.

Quite a large amount of data emerged from this research, and the author will only attempt to review some of the major findings. Twelve-person juries demonstrated more communication and deliberated longer than their six-person counterparts. Smaller juries, on an individual basis, made more comments than did twelve-person juries, and they allowed more equal sharing of communication. There were no differences between juror recall of arguments (conviction or acquittal) although six-person juries recalled a larger percentage of both kinds of arguments combined than did twelve-person juries. For both sized juries, the minority members felt they had significantly less influence on the process, experienced the deliberation process as less fair, and were rated by their fellow jurors as significantly less influential, less likable, and less reasonable than jurors in the majority.

An important dimension of the entire study had to do with the reliability of the verdicts rendered. For this factor, twelve-person juries appeared to be superior. For the college student sample, twelve-person juries were correct 83 percent of the time compared to 69 percent of the time for six-person juries. For the jury sample drawn from the former jurors of Franklin County, the numbers were 71 percent compared to 57 percent, once again favoring the larger-sized juries. Saks (1977) suggested that these comparisons were worth examining, notwithstanding the fact that the differences were not statistically significant. An important implication of the lesser reliability of six-person juries is stated by Saks (1977) as follows:

> —reduced jury size, while overall convicting fewer people, would convict more innocent and acquit more guilty defendants than larger juries, since the process that would produce this effects is reduced reliability, which is a consequence of the reduced jury size. (p. 88)

In addition, no differences were found in the number of hung juries, although other researchers have reported that twelve-person juries hang more often. In general, and as anticipated, the investigator found that the larger panels reflected a better representative cross-section of the community than the smaller panels. The reader may recall that the U. S. Supreme Court was very interested in this feature of jury trials in its opinions on jury size.

Moving to another key factor, Saks (1977) found that while quorum juries did not terminate deliberation as the minimum necessary votes became available, further deliberation had no effect on their ultimate verdicts. Not surprisingly, Saks' (1977) unanimous juries convicted with a greater sense of confidence in the defendants guilt than did quorum juries. No differences appeared in conviction-acquittal ratios or consistency between quorum and unanimous juries. The researcher did find that unanimous juries hung more often.

A majority of the research studies on jury decisionmaking processes have been determined to have such outstanding weaknesses that their value to the U. S. Supreme Court and other agencies is very questionable. Particularly misleading has been the work that attempted to shed light on six vs. twelve-member juries. Several studies yielded more valuable information to the courts. The ensuing chapters focus on other factors which contribute to jury behavior.

REFERENCES

Bermant, G. and Coppock, R. Outcomes of Six and Twelve Member Jury Trials: An analysis of 128 Civil Cases in the State of Washington. *Washington Law Review,* 1973, 48, 593-597.

Buckhout, R., Weg, C., Reilly, V., and Frohboese, R. Jury Verdicts: Comparison of 6 vs. 12 Person Juries and Unanimous vs. Majority Rule In a

Murder Trial. *Bulletin of the Psychonomic Society,* 1977, 10, 175-178.

Davis, J., Kerr, N., Atkins, R., Holt, R., and Meek, D. The Decision Processes of 6- and 12-Person Mock Juries Assigned Unanimous and Two-Thirds Majority Rules. *Journal of Personality and Social Psychology.* 1975, 32, 1-14.

Diamond, S. A Jury Experiment Reanalyzed. *University of Michigan Journal of Law Reform,* 1974, 7, 520-532.

Forston, R. The Decision-Making Process in the American Civil Jury: A Comparative Methodological Investigation. Unpublished doctoral dissertation, University of Minnesota, 1968.

Grofman, B. Not Necessarily Twelve and Not Necessarily Unanimous: Evaluating the Impact of *Williams v. Florida* and *Johnson v. Louisiana.* In G. Bermant, Nemeth, C., and Vidmar, N. *Psychology and the Law,* Lexington, MA: Lexington Books, 1975.

Institute of Judicial Administration. A Comparison of Six and Twelve Member Juries in New Jersey Superior and County Courts, 1972.

Kalven, H. and Zeisel, H. *The American Jury.* Chicago: The University of Chicago Press (Phoenix edition), 1971.

Kessler, J.B. The Social Psychology of Jury Deliberations. In R. J. Simon (ed.), *The Jury System In America.* Beverly Hills Sage Publications, 1975.

Kessler, J.B. An Empirical Study of Six and Twelve Member Jury Decision-Making Processes. *University of Michigan Journal of Law Reform,* 1973, 6, 712-734.

Lempert, R. Uncovering "Nondiscernible" Differences: Empirical Research and the Jury-Size Cases. *Michigan Law Review,* 1975, 73, 644-705.

Mills, L. Six-Member and Twelve-Member Juries: An Empirical Study of Trial Results. *University of Michigan Journal of Law Reform,* 1973, 6, 671-711.

Nemeth, C. Rules Governing Jury Deliberations: A Consideration of Recent Changes. In G. Bermant, Nemeth, C. and Vidmar, N. *Psychology and the Law.* Lexington, MA: Lexington Books, 1975.

Padawer-Singer, A., Singer, A., Singer, R. An Experimental Study of Twelve vs. Six Member Juries Under Unanimous vs. Nonunanimous Decisions. In B.D. Sales *Psychology in the Legal Process.* New York: Spectrum Publications, Inc., 1977.

Saks, M. *Jury Verdicts.* Lexington, MA: Lexington Books, 1977.

Valenti, A. and Downing, L. Differential Effects of Jury Size on Verdicts Following Deliberation As a Function of the Apparent Guilt of a Defendant. *Journal of Personality and Social Psychology,* 1975, 32, 655-663.

Williams v. Florida, 399 U.S. 78, *U.S. Supreme Court Reports,* 1970.

Zeisel, H. and Diamond, S. Convincing Empirical Evidence of the Six Member Jury. *University of Chicago Law Review,* 1974, 41, 281-295.

Chapter VI

CHARACTERISTICS OF JURORS, LITIGANTS AND WITNESSES

CHARACTERISTICS OF THE VARIOUS ACTORS are of more than passing interest, as their influence is frequently critical in the final decisions rendered by juries. Some defense lawyers go to unusual lengths to present their clients in the most favorable light, including their physical appearance and general demeanor in the courtroom. Kalven and Zeisel (1971) reported that certain factors associated with the defendant such as demonstrating kindness to the victim, inability to repeat the crime, an extended interval since the last conviction, and being a model prisoner contributed to leniency on the part of the jury.

In a case involving Representative Daniel Flood of Pennsylvania, the Congressman's age—he was seventy-five years old—was cited as the key factor in the holdout of one male juror (New York Times, 1979). Federal District Judge Oliver Basch declared a mistrial as the twelve-member jury was unable to reach a verdict, after deliberating for three days. One juror, Mrs. Johnnie Lyles, claimed that all efforts to influence the single juror had failed. Mrs. Lyles (New York Times, 1979) was quoted as saying, "He didn't want to hear anything. He said he knew Mr. Flood was guilty. But he would never vote guilty on anything, because Mr. Flood was too old" (p. D8).

The lawyer in a jury trial has a very significant role to play. Everyone recognizes this. What is not generally known is the degree to which his behavior and skill affect the outcome. Kalven and Zeisel's (1971) research factored out the impact of the attorney and they found that judges rated prosecution and defense as bal-

143

anced (essentially equal) in 78 percent of the cases, prosecution as superior in 13 percent of the cases, and defense superior in 11 percent of the cases. Embedded in these assessments were a number of observations offered by judges of counsels' skills, cleverness and behavior. The personality of a defendant's attorney in one case was noted by a judge who remarked:

> Defendant had not been in trouble before. He was defended by a young, honest and sincere lawyer who had known defendant before and believed the fantastic tale told by defendant. The honesty and decency of defense attorney rubbed off on the jurors who were hearing their first case. (p.364)

One interesting social psychological study that provides a backdrop for considering the interactions of the various functionaries was offered by Ekman and Friesen (1974). Jurors are constantly being challenged to judge the credibility of witnesses, defendants, and, of course, the attorneys themselves. In their study entitled "Detecting Deception From the Body or Face," the authors discovered that among subjects who had attempted to deceive, more mentioned attempting to disguise the face than the body. They stated that the results from testing their second hypothesis were "that when deceptive behavior was judged, more accurate judgments would be made from the body than from the face, but that when honest behavior was judged, there would be little difference in the accuracy achieved from the face or body was partially supported" (Ekman and Friesen, 1974, p. 288).

Many more empirical studies of litigants and jurors have been conducted than those of witnesses, but one study reported by Garcia and Griffitt (1978) found that the testimony of a likable witness had greater impact than that of a dislikable witness. In addition, the researchers reported that likable witnesses were believed more than dislikable witnesses. Subjects were eighty introductory psychology students and they read a description of the crime (an automobile pedestrian accident) followed by testimony presented by witnesses.

Following the witnesses' testimony, either five positive or five negative character traits—presented in narrative descriptions of the competence of the witnesses—were offered. Thus, while the results of the study are interesting, the nature of the methodology raises questions as to what degree the findings can be extended to actual jury situations. A simulation or dramatization of a trial, which included witness testimony on the stand, would have been greatly preferable. Also, of course, it should be possible to do field research on this topic in which actual courtroom trials provided a setting for data collection.

Miller et al. (1975) had role-played jurors exposed to the same testimony presented by a strong or weak witness. A professional actor played the part of both witnesses. The strong condition presented the witness as assertive, confident, and displaying few distracting nonverbal behaviors while the weak condition offered an image of the witness as unsure, halting, with nervous bodily and vocal behavior displayed. Jurors responded by rating both *credibility* and *retention of information* as superior for the strong witness.

Characteristics of Jurors

An interesting finding from a study conducted by Strodtbeck, James and Hawkins (1957) was that far fewer women were selected as jury foremen than would be expected by chance. In addition, they reported that, "Men, in contrast with women, and persons of higher in contrast with lower status occupations have higher participation, influence, satsfaction, and perceived competence for the jury task" (Strodtbeck, James, and Hawkins, 1957). The mock jurors employed in the study were drawn by lot from regular jury pools in Chicago and St. Louis courts.

Bevan et al. (1958) examined the impact of the prestige of the foreman in jury deliberations. In one case, the jury panels showed a greater increase in damages when the foreman was of lower prestige, but in a second study, the prestige of the foreman did not affect the amount of damages awarded by the mock juries. The foreman was a confederate of the experimenter.

While Simon (1967) reported a more equal sharing of participation in jury deliberations among males and females in her second study, an earlier investigation revealed that males participated more actively. In the earlier study (James, 1959) she also reported that participation varied according to education attained, with those who had achieved more education participating more often. However, no differences were found between the more and less educated jurors in their ability either to influence other members or to be persuaded by them. Jurors spent 50 percent of the time discussing personal experiences, 25 percent of the time on procedural matters, 15 percent reviewing the facts of the case, and 8 percent on the judge's instructions.

Returning to her later study, in criminal cases involving a defense of insanity, black jurors were more willing to vote for acquittal than jurors of majority ethnic background or jurors of higher educational status (Simon, 1967). But social status and occupational characteristics have a limited effect upon a juror's behavior and as Simon (1967) has noted:

> It is extremely difficult to predict the response or behavior of a given individual to a concrete situation on the basis of such gross characteristics as occupation, education, sex or age. In any situation what a person thinks or does is a function of who he is, the exigencies of the situation, how strongly he feels about the problem, and a host of other factors. (p. 118)

In England, Sealy and Cornish (1973) were also interested in various characteristics of jurors and their effects upon decision-making. The most "striking" finding was that there was a positive relationship between the youth of the jurors and their verdicts. In the two trials studied, no relationships were demonstrated between the occupational and educational status of the jurors and their tendency to convict.

Seven hundred jurors were interviewed in Colorado by Bronson (1970) in his study of conviction proneness and attitudes toward capital punishment. Those who more strongly favored the death penalty were more likely to vote for conviction. The author states, "While the difference in conviction proneness between those who favor and oppose the death penalty is not overwhelming, it is consistent, predictable, and substantial" (p. 31). Questionnaire data were used as a basis for determining the subjects' attitudes.

Other work in this area includes studies by Boehm (1938), Crosson (1967), Wilson (1964), Jurow (1971), Mitchell and

Byrne (1973), and Berg and Vidmar (1975). Boehm (1968) focused on the relationship of guilt and authoritarianism. College subjects were asked to reach a verdict in a manslaughter case. Findings were that subjects who presented authoritarian attitudes judged a defendant guilty more often than those who were non-authoritarian. Crosson's (1967) work relied on jurors involved in capital cases, as well as jurors who had served on noncapital cases. Those who were "death qualified" demonstrated more politically conservative attitudes than their counterparts. No differences between the groups were found on scales measuring dogmatism, critical thinking, and general hostility. Brief outlines of evidence in six simulated capital cases were provided to 187 college students by Wilson (1964). He concluded, not surprisingly, that subjects who indicated that they had conscientious scruples against the death penalty offered guilty verdicts significantly less often than did subjects who had no such concerns.

Jurow (1971) reported on jurors who favored capital punishment. They were industrial workers who appeared to be comparable to persons chosen from the ranks of actual juror pools. He found that there was a positive relationship between favorable attitudes toward capital punishment and politically conservative attitudes, authoritarianism and punitiveness. The author (Jurow, 1971) noted:

> . . . although we can speculate on variables, personality or others, that affect a juror's tendency to conflict or acquit, the best approach is the most direct one. The Legal Attitudes Questionnaire asks subjects whether they agree or disagree with such statements as, "too many obviously guilty persons escape punishment because of legal technicalities," or, "upstanding citizens have nothing to fear from the police." (p. 593)

Mitchell and Byrne (1973) found that high authoritarians were more guilt oriented than law authoritarians in regard to a defendant with dissimilar attitudes. Among the 139 subjects, those who were more authoritarian were also found to be more punitive toward a dissimilar defendant. The work of Kerr and Anderson (1978) was also concerned with defendant-juror similarity. They hypothesized that juror-defendant similarity, defined with respect to group religious membership, would lead to greater leniency toward the defendant when the evidence was weak, but when the evidence was strong, it was expected that the relationship would be the opposite. Subjects were Christian and Jewish students who role-played jurors. They responded to cases in which Christian or Jewish defendants encountered strong or weak evidence against them. They reported a positive relationship between religious similarity and the evaluation of the defendant and leniency. However, the relationship was not affected by the strength of evidence against the defendant as the authors had predicted. Also, Jewish subjects were more lenient than Christian subjects.

Berg and Vidmar (1975) found that more authoritarian subjects are more accurate at remembering evidence about the defendant's character, while low authoritarians recall more of the situational evidence.

Another study that looked at characteristics of defendants and jurors was reported by Nemeth and Sosis (1973). Their results indicated that conservative jurors gave more severe sentences to an unattractive defendant but attractiveness was unrelated to judgments of liberal jurors. Furthermore, white defendants were offered lighter sentences from liberal jurors than from conservative jurors, but no significant differences were reported for black defendants.

Characteristics of Litigants

For years, people have speculated concerning the value of being physically attractive. Social scientists have demonstrated that benefits do indeed accrue to the beautiful. Landy and Aronson (1969), employing mock jurors, found that when the defendant was perceived as attractive, he or she received a lighter sentence than when the defendant was perceived as unattractive. Stephan and Tully (1973) reported a similar finding favoring the attractive. Attractive plaintiffs in a personal injury suit had a higher recovery rate and received greater financial compensation than unattractive plaintiffs. In a study undertaken by Efran (1974), subjects were given case summaries and a photograph of an attractive or unattractive defendant of the opposite sex. Mock jurors were required to make determinations of guilt and administer a sentence. The researcher reported that males rated the attractive defendants less guilty and responded less punitively. On the other hand, the reactions of female subjects differed as significant relationships were not found on these variables.

Sigall and Ostrove (1973) also investigated attractiveness in defendants. After reading a case account, subjects sentenced defendants to a period of incarceration. They hypothesized that when the crime was unrelated to attractiveness i.e. burglary, subjects would assign more lenient sentences to the attractive defendant. They also predicted the corollary: when the crime was related to attractiveness, i.e. a swindle, the attractive defendant would receive a less lenient response. Generally, the authors found support for their expectations.

Group discussion was found to affect responses of mock jurors to attractive and unattractive defendants (Izzett and Leginski, 1974). Subjects read a case concerning a negligent automobile homicide. They read identical versions of the case, but in one instance, the defendant was attractive while in the other case, the person was unattractive. After subjects were asked to sentence the defendants, group discussions were held. Prior to group discussion, subjects had presented longer sentences to the unattractive defendant. Following group discussion, the subjects offered more lenient sentences to the unattractive defendant while no significant change was reported for the attractive defendant.

Another quality that was examined was the *respectability* of the victim (Jones and Aronson, 1973). The experimenters arranged for subjects to respond to a rape case in which (a) the victim was presented as more respectable (a virgin or married) or (b) less respectable (divorced). They assumed that individuals would perceive the divorced woman as less respectable and therefore the defendant would be sentenced to a shorter period than in the other condition. Also, they took the position that "the more respectable the victim, the greater the need to attribute fault to his character." The results supported the authors' speculations with subjects faulting the victim more if she was married or a virgin than when she was divorced. Longer sentences were meted out to the defendant when he was viewed as raping the married woman or virgin.

For scholars working in this field of psychology-law, there is always the nagging question as to what extent the findings of simulations and other laboratory studies apply to the real world. Wilson and Donnerstein (1977) tackled this question by comparing groups of subjects, described as *real consequences* subjects and *hypothetical consequences* subjects. They found that indeed there were differences. Real consequences subjects were told that their assistance was needed in deciding what should be done in a real case involving a student suspected of having taken and then distributed the questions to an exam. They were told that the instructor did not wish to decide himself. Hypothetical consequences subjects were asked to participate in an experiment dealing with the student judicial process. In real consequences, the likelihood of conviction was greater. The authors note that including their own two experiments, four studies now exist which indicate a difference in conviction rates between subjects under real and hypothetical consequences conditions. Also, under real consequences, offender character attractiveness did not affect conviction rates, although in the hypothetical consequences subjects it was a factor. In their second experiment, the physical attractiveness of the offender did not influence either group of subjects. While it is obviously important that at least some scholars concern themselves with the linkages between laboratory research and the real world, in this study the title is misleading: "Guilty or Not Guilty? A Look at the 'Simulated' Jury Paradigm." The researchers under their *real consequences* condition hardly replicated a real-life jury situation. They attempted, perhaps successfully, to lead one group of subjects to believe that their opinions involved responses to a real-life circumstance, but that was quite different than what real jurors experience in a real trial with genuine deliberations.

An important characteristic of defendants that frequently makes its way into headline news stories is the emotional stability of the person. If the person is described as a "psychiatric" or "mental" case, journalists are sure to pick up on it. Smith, Sue and Padilla (1976) researched this question. They also introduced a second variable of a violent or nonviolent crime. For simulated jurors, the "former mental patient" received fewer guilty verdicts than did the nonhospitalized defendant in the non-violent condition, but no differences were found for the violent (robbery) condition.   The researchers suggest that "the result seems to reflect a tolerant or sympathetic orientation toward the previously hospitalized defendant when he was accused of a 'crime against property'." But in the robbery assault condition, a different attitude was presented by subjects; tolerance disappeared when violence was involved.

This chapter has examined the way in which the characteristics of the functionaries affects trial outcomes.   The evidence suggests clearly that emotional and behavioral responses have a far greater impact on the merits of any given case than is generally recognized.   The notion of a carefully controlled environment in which evidence is presented and discussed in an unbiased fashion is deeply flawed.

REFERENCES

Berg, K. and Vidmar, N.   Authoritarianism and Recall of Evidence About Criminal Behavior.   *Journal of Research in Personality,* 1975, 9, 147-157.

Bevan, W., Albert, R., Loiseux, P., Mayfield, P., and Wright, G.   Jury Behavior As a Function of the Prestige of the Foreman and the Nature of his Leadership.   *Journal of Public Law,* 1958, 7, 419-449.

Boehm, V.   Mr. Prejudice, Miss Sympathy, and the Authoritarian Personality: An Application of Psychological Measuring Techniques to the Problem of Jury Bias.   *Wisconsin Law Review,* 1968, 734-750.

Bronson, E.   On the Conviction Proneness and Representativeness of the Death-Qualified Jury: An Empirical Study of Colorado Veniremen.   *University of Colorado Law Review,* 1970, 42, 1-32.

Crosson, R.F.   An Investigation Into Certain Personality Variables Among Capital Trial Jurors.   *Dissertation Abstracts,* 1967, 27, 3668B-3669B.

Efran, M.   The Effects of Physical Appearance on the Judgment of Guilt. Interpersonal Attraction, and Severity of Recommended Punishment in a Simulated Jury Task. *Journal of Research in Personality,* 1974, 8, 45-54.

Ekman, P. and Friesen, W.   Detecting Deception From the Body or Face. *Journal of Personality and Social Psychology,* 1974, 29, 288-298.

Garcia, L. and Griffitt, W.   Impact of Testimonial Evidence as a Function of Witness Characteristics.   *Bulletin of the Psychonomic Society,* 1978, 11, 37-40.

Izzett, R. and Leginski, W.   Group Discussion and the Influence of Defendant Characteristics in a Simulated Jury Setting.   *Journal of Social Psychology,* 1974, 93, 271-279.

James, R. Status and Competence in Jury Deliberations. *American Journal of Sociology*, 1959, 64, 563-570.

Jones, C. and Aronson, E. Attribution of Fault to a Rape Victim as a Function of Respectability of the Victim. *Journal of Personality and Social Psychology*, 1973, 26, 415-419.

Jurow, G. New Data on the Effect of a "Death Qualified" Jury on the Guilt Determination Process. *Harvard Law Review*, 1971, 84, 567-611.

Kalven, H. and Zeisel, H. *The American Jury*. Chicago: The University of Chicago Press (Phoenix edition), 1971.

Kerr, N. and Anderson, A. Defendant-Juror Religious Similarity and Mock Jurors' Judgments. Paper presented at the American Psychological Association Convention, September 1, 1978, Toronto, Ontario, Canada.

Landy, D. and Aronson, E. The Influence of the Character of the Criminal and his Victim on the Decisions of Simulated Jurors. *Journal of Experimental Social Psychology*, 1969, 5, 141-152.

Miller, G.R., Boster, F.J., Fontes, N.E., LeFebvre, D.J. and Poole, M.S. Jurors' Responses To Videotaped Trial Materials—Some Further Evidence. *Michigan State Bar Journal*, 1975, 54, 278-282.

Mitchell, H. and Byrne, D. The Defendant's Dilemma: Effects of Jurors' Attitudes and Authoritarianism on Judicial Decisions. *Journal of Personality and Social Psychology*, 1973, 25, 123-129.

Nemeth, C. and Sosis, R. A Simulated Jury Study: Characteristics of the Defendant and the Jurors. *Journal of Social Psychology*, 1973, 90, 221-229.

New York Times, "Juror Who Opposed Conviction of Flood Assailed By a Colleague," February 5, 1979, p. D8.

Sealy, A., and Cornish, W. Jurors and Their Verdicts. *Modern Law Review*, 1973, 36, 496-508.

Sigall, H. and Ostrove, N. Effects of the Physical Attractiveness of the Defendant and Nature of the Crime on Juridic Judgment. Paper presented at the American Psychological Association, Montreal, 1973.

Simon, R. *The Jury and the Defense of Insanity Boston:* Little Brown & Company, 1967.

Smith, R., Sue, S. and Padilla, E. Effects of a Defendant's Previous Psychiatric Hospitalization on the Judgments of Simulated Jurors. *American Journal of Community Psychology*, 1976, 4, 133-144.

Stephan, C. and Tully, J. The Influence of Physical Attriveness of a Plaintiff on the Decisions of Simulated Jurors. Paper read at the North Central Sociological Association, Cincinnati, Ohio, 1973.

Strodtbeck, F., James, R. and Hawkins, C. Social Status In Jury Deliberations. *The American Sociological Review*, 1957, 22, 713-719.

Wilson, W. Belief in Capital Punishment and Jury Performances. Cited in G. Jurow, New Data on the Effect of a "Death Qualified" Jury On the Guilt Determination Process. *Harvard Law Review*, 1971, 84, 567-611.

Wilson, D. and Donnerstein, E. Guilty or Not Guilty? A Look at the "Simulated" Jury Paradigm. *Journal of Applied Social Psychology*, 1972, 7, 175-190.

Chapter VII

VIDEOTAPED PRESENTATIONS AND PRETRIAL PUBLICITY

VIDEOTAPING OF LEGAL PROCEEDINGS

THE AVAILABILITY of an economically efficient method of repro-
ducing testimony in courtroom proceedings has resulted in
a wave of unrest among legal scholars and members of the judiciary.
The opinions on the videotaping of testimony range from essentially an all-out endorsement of its value (Miller, 1976) to apprehension that social scientists' research on this subject will result in
revolutionary changes in courtroom practices that may evade the
legal establishments' scrutiny (Grow and Johnson, 1975). In
addition to questions such as the editorial power of the manager,
quality of reproduction, overall impact on viewers, and the restricted or unrestricted use of the medium, there are questions concerning the constitutionality of such endeavors.

At least one legal scholar (Stiver, 1974) foresees no insur-
mountable problems in this respect. He reviewed questions related to the due process clause of the U. S. Constitution which requires that *a trial be fair,* that a person has *a right to a public trial,*
and *a right to a trial by jury.* In all these instances, he reports that
videotaping, within limits, can pass constitutional muster. This
author is not nearly as sanguine as Stiver, particularly on the point
concerning the fairness of a trial. In anticipation of research
evidence to be reviewed in this section, which bears directly on the
problem of live vs. videotaped presentations, it should be noted
that "the votes have not all been counted." Too few studies have
been conducted which approach this problem directly.

Initial evidence is far from clear on the matter of juror respon-

153

siveness to taped vs. live trials (Farmer, Williams, Lee, Cundick, Howell and Rooker, 1976). If additional social-psychological experimental evidence demonstrates differences, then a litigant may well have a valid argument that his videotaped trial (or portions of it) was unfair.

Stiver (1974) stressed that since the Founders' intent in providing the *right to public trial* is unclear, the constitutionality of videotaped proceedings must be gleaned from case law and that the two main functions appear to be (1) "the prevention of governmental persecution: the state is less likely to prosecute without justification when its actions are open to public scrutiny," and (2) "to motivate trial participants to regard their responsibilities more seriously" (p. 621). In neither case, he suggests, does conducting videotaped trials need to interfere with these functions.

On the matter of the *right to trial by jury,* Stiver (1974) directed his attention at the "operational" purposes of the jury trial and indicated that the purposes include: (1) the interposition between the accused and his accuser of the commonsense judgment of a group of laymen, (2) the community participation and shared responsibility that results from that group's determination of guilt or innocence, (3) the jury must be large enough to ensure deliberation, (4) must be free from attempts at intimidation, and (5) must provide a fair possibility for obtaining a representative cross-section of the community. Again, he perceived no overwhelming problems from the use of videotaped testimony meeting these requirements.

In general, the arguments for the use of videotape include economy, preservation of testimony, clarity, ability to delete inadmissible evidence, and the opportunity to take depositions immediately after the event. Some of these factors are appealing to those concerned with heavily crowded court calendars because there is intense pressure to relieve the burdensome load. Concerning the matter of saving court time, Farmer et al. (1976) have noted:

> There are several arguments supporting the idea that videotape trials would save court time. For example, it is argued that by video-taping the evidence and then previewing this record in advance, the lawyers could probably come to agreement on some disputed evi-

dentiary questions. That way, the judge would not have to be there
at the presentation of the evidence to the jury. Jury time is also
saved, principally by the elimination of delays while the court and
counsel resolve evidentiary and procedural matters. (p. 210).

Not only would there be a convenience factor involved in the
taking of a deposition by videotape, but this might prove crucial
for a witness geographically far removed from the location of the
trial. And what about a critically injured witness who is hospitalized? The need for immediate access to this person's testimony is
apparent. The problem of bias and prejudice associated with eyewitness testimony, including the administration of lineups, has
been discussed at length elsewhere in this volume. The videotaping of lineups would provide some assurance to judge and jury
that blatant prejudice had at least been controlled during that
stage. Stiver (1974) observed that videotape lends itself to the
recording of expert testimony and the presentation of confessions
of defendants in criminal cases.

Among the scant number of studies undertaken to examine the
effect of videotaped proceedings are a series reported by Miller
(1976) and his colleagues at Michigan State University. They are
also among the most controversial and have not been immune
from criticism. The Michigan State University group was interested in examining the overall effects of videotaped trials versus
live trials. In one of their studies (Miller, Bender, Florence and
Nicholson, 1974), they drew on fifty-two jurors from the Genesee
County Circuit Court in Flint, Michigan. The researchers arranged for some jurors to observe the trial live while others
viewed it on tape. Miller's (1976) report of the study stated,
"When compared with their counterparts who viewed a live trial,
jurors who viewed the videotaped trial arrived at similar judgments about negligence and amount of award, had similar perceptions of the contesting attorneys, retained as much of the trial-
related information, and reported similar levels of interest and
motivation toward the task of serving as jurors" (p. 191). However, in this case, which involved contributory negligence on the
part of the plaintiff, the results of the different exposures may
have included some differences. Farmer et al. (1976) report that
in a reanalysis of the data "a consistent trend in Miller's data was

noted when the verdicts of all of the jury panels which viewed the trial on videotape were examined. The pattern of preferred verdicts resulting from the video trial was consistently different from that of the live trial verdicts" (p. 211). The failure of Miller et al. to identify a precise level of significance in their statistical testing and reporting of "no differences" between the live vs. videotaped presentations does not inspire confidence in their work.

Clearly a major issue posed by the application of videotape technology in the courtroom has to do with the decisions to video-tape certain events at the expense of others. If the camera takes in the entire courtroom scene, much detail will be lost. These decisions not only involve the camera choices exercised at the time the original event is taped, but they extend to the editorial process as well. Not all material can be included. A closeup shot, by definition, excludes the recording of the wider panorama of activity. The use of multiple cameras does not obviate the problem, but merely diminishes it. While the "split screen" technique theoretically allows the viewer to react to more than one secne, it, too, has its limitations. The viewer may be concentrating on one image and totally ignore the companion image presented. For example, imagine a juror in a "live" case who may observe the pained expression of the defendant upon his hearing of damaging evidence cited against him, compared to his counterpart viewing the same trial on videotape who may be denied the opportunity of viewing the defendant at that moment.

Even if a camera happens to be focused on the defendant at the critical moment, there is no guarantee that his ashen complexion will be fully and accurately conveyed to those viewing a T.V. monitor, notwithstanding the fact that the most sophisticated color system may be in use. It is hard to imagine how a videotaped image could ever replace the advantages of viewing the person in the flesh and blood. The subtleties and nuances of facial expressions, coloring, etc. may elude the most advanced technical system. Granted, in a given instance, a juror might benefit from a closeup video shot of a witness that might escape him in the actual situation, due to his physical distance from the person, or because his view is obscured, but this is not apt to be the case, given the usual proximity of the jury to the courtroom action.

A second study by the Michigan State Group (Miller, 1976) investigated the impact of a split-screen system with that of a full screen system. The split-screen technique employed a triple camera and presented close-ups of the witness, the inquiring attorney and the judge. Subjects were fifty-seven adult members of a Catholic church group in Michigan who role-played jurors. They were either assigned to the full screen or split-screen condition. In addition, they were exposed to the same trial *(Nugent v. Clark)* that had been presented in the first study.

While the authors report no differences between the jurors who viewed the trial on the split-screen system compared to those who watched on the full-screen apparatus for either the negligence verdicts or the awards of Mr. and Mrs. Nugent, perceptions of attorney credibility appeared to have been affected. Surprisingly, the researchers appeared to dismiss this matter (Miller, 1976) by suggesting "it is less than overwhelming, since the difference is significant for only the plaintiff's attorney" (p. 194). Later on, they appear to have minimized once again differences that cropped up in their data by stating, "Finally, the data reveal no clear indication that jurors were differentially interested or motivated in the two conditions, though there is a trend toward higher self-report ratings of interest and motivation in the split-screen condition (X, split screen = S. 3; ×, full screen = 4.94; t = 1.52; p < 10)" (p. 194).

In a further study of *inadmissible testimony*, Miller (1976) reported on a project which included 120 jurors who served on the Wayne Circuit Court jury panel (Michigan). They were variously assigned to conditions which ranged from zero deletions of inadmissible testimony to six deletions of inadmissible testimony. Perhaps surprisingly, the researchers reported no evidence that either the factor of negligence verdicts nor awards was affected by the amount of inadmissible evidence.

In another phase of their research, this group (Miller, 1976) compared the amount of information retained in live, color, and black-and-white videotaped presentations. They also examined physiological arousal stimulated by color and black-and-white taped presentations (Galvanic Skin Response) along with credibility ratings of participants in the two videotaped conditions. They report that information retention was greatest for the black-and-white videotape condition, followed by color videotape and then the live condition. Arousal was greater in the black-and-white taped condition than in the color-taped condition. In conclusion, the authors point out that for the color videotape approach, the credibility of witnesses and attorneys was greater than in the black-and-white exposure. The authors note that a perplexing finding was that subjects exposed to monochromatic (black-and-white) viewing retained more trial-related information than those exposed to color viewing.

Bermant, Chappell, Crockett, Jacovbovitch and McGuire (1975) studied jurors in Ohio and California. Ohio had witnessed a pioneering effort on the part of Judge James McCrystal in exploring the use of large segments of taped testimony for use in jury trials. With the taping of extensive amounts of testimony, objectionable material can be edited out. After providing extensive trial testimony for videotaped viewing, a procedure described as prerecorded videotape trial presentation (PRVTT), the response of California jurors was studied in a case identified as *Liggons v. Haniske*. A second phase of the study involved a large scale mail survey of jurors in Ohio.

Generally, the authors report favorable responses from the subjects surveyed as to the use of videotape in the courtroom. However, the responses were far from uniform, and an "impersonal" quality characterized the reactions of some jurors. For instance, one who was highly critical was quoted as saying:

> Feeling [for the witnesses] was definitely completely lost. I didn't have any more feeling for either one of those people—just of the words that they had said—which a friend of mine was arguing for, saying, well that's good, you weren't influenced by their personalities. On the other hand, their personalities are why they are the people they are. It's really hard to tell where you draw the line in that kind of situation and what on T.V. should be acceptable and what should not be. (p. 986)

Another remarked that, "It's just very hard to explain—the human factor is needed. It's just as if all of a sudden we are all becoming numbers" (p. 87).

A number of jurors, however, responded in a positive vein noting that fewer distractions were present in the televised proceeding and that a more "relaxed" atmosphere prevailed. Although there was disagreement as to whether or not the relaxed atmosphere allowed jurors to obtain a better understanding of the veracity of the witnesses.

In summing up their findings, the researchers (Bermant, Chappell, Crockett, Jacovbovitch and McGuire, 1975) stated that a majority of both the California and Ohio subjects would choose videotape for a civil trial in which they were litigants. They were less optimistic regarding a criminal trial. Strong opposition to the use of PRVTT in a criminal proceeding was voiced by the California jurors: "They expressed their view that when the liberty of the accused was at stake, the courtroom drama should be played to a live audience by a live company of actors." In the Ohio sample, 76 percent of jurors had indicated that they would opt for videotape in a civil case, while only 43 percent indicated that they would choose videotape for a criminal trial in which they were defendants.

For research investigators, a familiar issue arises: "the study raises more questions than it answers." It would be interesting to have a more detailed understanding of the attitudes of the jurors studied and why there was such a contrast between their responses to civil and criminal cases. The reactions appear to be so mixed that the researchers' general statement mentioned earlier—that overall the responses were favorable—seems unwarranted.

Research by Farmer et al. (1976) represents one of the better research efforts in this area. They drew on a case which involved a land condemnation action. Jurors were drawn from lists of persons who had previously served as district court jurors in Utah County (State of Utah). The results indicated that the *transcript trial* was rated as significantly less stimulating than the *live trial* on all five dimensions studied. In addition, as far as the live trial was concerned, the *audio trial* was rated as significantly less arousing and the *color trial* as even less stimulating. The *black-and-white trial*, however, was not significantly different from the live trial. Reactions varied a great deal to the different witnesses and these varied responses appeared to interact with the medium. The researchers presented a skeptical view of the videotaped trial in offering suggestions for future research:

> The most serious potential impact of these differences is that they may influence the outcome of trials. Jurors may plausibly be led by these different perceptions to render a different verdict or to vary the amount of dollars or quality of awards. This potential biasing effect of videotape presentations of trial testimony suggests the need for research specifically designed to compare deliberated jury verdicts after live and media presentations of the same trial testimony repeated over a number of trials using several witnesses and attorney types. (p. 235)

One scholarly piece of analysis on videotape in the courtroom was offered by Doret (1974). At one point he directed his attention to the role of the judge in videotaped trial proceedings, and he raised the question of the importance of the presence of the judge during testimony taking. The Ohio trials pioneered by Mc-Crystal, and mentioned earlier, involved the taping of testimony without the presence of the judge. Doret (1974), however favors the presence of the judge in the taping of testimony for the following reasons:

(1) The judge helps to establish an atmosphere of "dignity" and his presence enhances the cooperativeness of the various parties, including counsel, during testimony-taking;

(2) A judge is required to make rulings on contested points of relevance, prejudice, admissibility, etc;

(3) Absence of the judge might encourage the participants to request "retakes," if the examination did not go well.

As he observes: "The jury must continue to be able to see, in its spontaneous form, the surprise or embarrassment of a witness when the unexpected occurs. Such spontaneity is clearly an aid to truthfinding. In addition, unless retakes were prohibited, lawyers might feel that they need not present their best effort on the first taping" (p. 238).

As this writer has previously remarked, the videotaping process may filter out some of the expressiveness of those on camera, but the larger question of the impact of the reduced courtroom drama is again raised. *It appears that the power generated by the live trial is embedded in the atmosphere—including the presence of judge and jury. To strip away the various functionaries may well reduce the psychological force that aids in truthfinding.*

Returning to Doret's (1974) work, he points out potential problems of the videotaped trial by examining the way *information* available to the jury is affected:

> There will be: (1) a loss of the completeness in the information communicated, (2) an electronic distortion of the information communicated, (3) a limiting in the information carrying capacity of the trial, (4) perceptual distortions in the information communicated, (5) a loss in the veracity of the information communicated and (6) an innate biasing of the information communicated. (p. 241)

In a survey of judges and attorneys, Grow and Johnson (1975) uncovered some resistance on the part of these members of the legal establishment. In general, respondents reacted negatively to many characteristics of videotape that are perceived as assets by proponents. Among a list of characteristics of a videotape trial, the following were seen as the most *advantageous:* (1) testimony may be taken at a time convenient to the witnesses and attorneys (42%); (2) cost savings to the parties (41%). The combined sample of judges and attorneys rated the following as most *disadvantageous:* (1) jurors perceive such character traits as honesty, friendliness, nervousness, objectivity, and appearance differently in a videotape trial than in a live trial (50%); (2) videotaping reduces the public's sense that the jury trial is a legitimate means of conflict resolution (36%).

In a report prepared for the National Center for State Courts, Taillefer, Short, Greenwood, and Brady (1974) highlighted the importance of the technical and production side by stating, "The operator controlling the video recording and the type of equipment used has great potential for influencing juror or judicial perceptions of the testimony" (p. 118).

PRETRIAL PUBLICITY

Pretrial publicity has continued to occupy the attention of jurists and legal scholars with a number of recent court decisions fueling the controversy. Saks and Hastie (1978) commented on the trial of Susan Saxe in Massachusetts. As a political revolutionary from the Vietnam war era, her case received a great deal of attention in the local press—much of it unfavorable to the defense. Research conducted prior to her trial revealed that 75 percent of the adult population living in the county where she was to be tried believed her to be guilty. Appparently in response to this situation, the trial judge granted the defense lawyers extra peremptory challenges of jurors in an effort to counteract pretrial publicity (Hastie and Saks, 1978) .

In New York recently, Chief Judge Irving Kaufman of the United States Court of Appeals for the Second Circuit was very critical of New York's Appellate Courts for not analyzing carefully the case of a burglary suspect who had complained that he had been convicted by a jury that had read a newspaper article (Lubasch, 1978) . Among the comments offered by Judge Kaufman were the following, "The modern jury is instructed to reach its verdict solely on the basis of the evidence before it." He went on to say, "This sensitivity to the source of information brought into the jury room is grounded in the unremarkable perception that all evidence developed against an accused must come from the witness stand in a public courtroom, where there is full protection of the defendant's right of confrontation, of cross-examination and of counsel."

A number of researchers have investigated the issue of pretrial publicity using a mock jury paradigm (Simon, 1966; Kline and Jess, 1966) , but the now familiar problem of the researchers employing subjects who appear unlike bona fide jurors is raised. Upper middle-class volunteers and college students were drawn upon in the above-mentioned projects.

Buckhout et al. (1973) reported on a problem of pretrial publicity in Albany County. The social science staff of the Center for Responsive Psychology attempted to assist in the case of a Mr. Stephen LaRose. Extensive articles, which appeared in the *Albany Times Union* and the *Knickerbocker-News Union-Star,* which the staff viewed as damaging to the defendant, were considered. A survey of individuals "who were representative of persons likely to be selected as jurors" was then undertaken in Albany County. Of the 212 persons surveyed, who were either present jurors at that time or former jurors, 89.2 percent stated that they were familiar with the case.

Another question which asked the subjects to respond to the assumed guilt of LaRose elicited a relatively high score (5.95 on a scale of 10) when compared with the names of other defendants mentioned in the survey. Although considerable additional information was presented to the court by Buckhout (1973) in the form of a deposition, all of which pointed to significant prejudicial pretrial publicity, the motion by LaRose's attorney requesting a change of venue was denied.

Sue and Smith (1974) reported on the pretrial publicity problem in conjunction with two studies they undertook. In the first study, 105 university students were presented with a description of a grocery store robbery. They were also offered information concerning the suspect's apprehension by police and a summary of evidence presented by each side at the trial. Half the students received strong evidence against the defendant, while half received weak evidence. In addition, some members of each group received added "incriminating evidence" that was declared either admissible or inadmissible. A control group was also employed.

In reporting their results, Sue and Smith (1974) state, "It appears that the biasing effect of inadmissable evidence is greatest when there is little other evidence on which to make a decision. The controversial evidence then becomes quite salient in a juror's mind. On the other hand, when there is already strong evidence against the defendant, the inadmissible evidence seems to have little effect on a juror's verdict" (p. 90).

In the second study, the investigators included responses of 100 community residents in addition to the 105 college students. Also, verdicts were compared with those who had received judicial instructions to disregard pretrial publicity to those subjects who were exposed to a "neutral judicial statement." When examining the results, the researchers (Sue and Smith, 1974) report that females voted guilty more than males. Also, they found that the impact of the adverse but inadmissible pretrial publicity had affected the mock jurors' subsequent evaluation of evidence presented at the trial. Furthermore, it encouraged guilty verdicts and increased subjects' ratings of how convincing the prosecutor's case was.

The most important study to date, undertaken to examine the

question of "free press—fair trial," was that conducted by Padawer-Singer and Barton (1975). The study included real jurors employing a tape-recorded murder case in which the jurors were instructed to deliberate to a verdict.

The first phase of the study was actually conducted at the Supreme Court of the State of New York in Mineola, while the second phase took place at Kings County Supreme Court in Brooklyn. In the first phase, one group of jurors was exposed to newspaper clippings which contained material reporting on the defendant's prior record and withdrawn confession, while a second group received neutral press clippings. The results of the first project were that in the biased condition, forty-seven out of sixty juries decided the defendant was guilty, while in the unbiased condition, thirty-three out of sixty juries determined the defendant was guilty.

While much like the first phase, the second phase of the research project included a factor of voir dire (jury selection) examination. It was offered to half of those in the biased condition while the other half of those in the biased condition were chosen by random selection from the general pool of jurors. A predeliberation ballot was also presented in this experiment along with extended time for jury deliberations. Generally, the results were similar to the first phase; the prejudicial press clippings influenced juries to offer more guilty verdicts—six out of ten compared with two out of thirteen. Overall, 69 percent of those who participated in the prejudicial condition compared with only 35 percent in the nonprejudiced condition voted guilty. Thus, the general conclusion from both phases was that the prejudicial material had a powerful effect upon jurors' behavior.

Summary

This chapter has been concerned with two phenomena that impact on the jury: videotaped presentations and pretrial publicity. The present use of videotape in the courtroom was found to be somewhat promising, yet at the same time there appeared to be serious limitations to the technique. Among other things, the emotional flavor of the participants and their interactions may be siphoned off through the use of videotape technology. Regarding pretrial publicity, while the courts and the press have had a great deal to say about this matter, a dearth of psychological research exists presently on the subject. Studies that have been done support the notion that it can have a strong prejudicial effect on trials.

REFERENCES

Bermant, G., Chappell, D., Crockett, M., Jacovbovitch, M. and McGuire, M. Juror Responses to Prerecorded Videotape Presentations in California and Ohio. *Hastings Law Journal,* 1975, 26, 975-998.

Buckhout, R., Weg, S., Cohen, R., and Becker, R. Case Study of the Presumption of Guilt by Jurors. Center for Responsive Psychology, Brooklyn College, CR-8, December 1, 1973.

Doret, D. Trial By Videotape—Can Justice Be Seen to Be Done? *Temple Law Quarterly,* 1974, 47, 228-268.

Farmer, L., Williams, G., Lee, R., Cundick, B., Howell, R., Rooker, C. Juror Perceptions of Trial Testimony As a Function of the Method of Presentation. In G. Bermant, C. Nemeth, and N. Vidman (Eds.), *Psychology and the Law,* Lexington, MA: D. C. Heath and Company, 1976.

Farmer, L., Williams, G., Cundick, B., Howell, R., Lee, R. and Rooker, C. The Effect of the Method of Presenting Trial Testimony on Juror Decisional Processes. In B. Sales (Ed.) *Psychology In the Legal Process,* New York: Spectrum Publications, Inc., 1977.

Grow, R. and Johnson, R. Opening Pandora's Box: Asking Judges and Attorneys to React to the Videotape Trial. *Brigham Young Law Review,* 1975, 2, 487-527.

Kline, F. and Jess, P. Prejudicial Publicity: Its Effect on Law School Mock Juries. *Journalism Quarterly,* 1966, 43, 113-116.

Lubasch, A. Defendant Is Upheld On A Faulty Verdict. *New York Times,* May 6, 1978.

Miller, G. The Effects of Videotaped Trial Materials on Juror Response. In G. Bermant, C. Nemeth, and N. Vidman (Eds.), *Psychology and the Law,* Lexington, MA: D. C. Heath and Company, 1976.

Miller, G., Bender, D., Florence, T. and Nicholson, H. Real Versus Reel: What's the Verdict. *Journal of Communication,* 1974, 24, 99-111.

Padawer-Singer, A., and Barton, A. The Impact of Pretrial Publicity. In R. J. Simon (Ed.), *The Jury System in America.* Beverly Hills: Sage Publications, 1975.

Saks, M. and Hastie, R. *Social Psychology in Court.* New York: Van Nostrand Reinhold Company, 1978.

Simon, R. Murder, Juries and the Press. *Transaction,* 1966, 3, 40-42.

Stiver, C. Video-Tape Trials: A Practical Evaluation and a Legal Analysis. *Stanford Law Review*, 1974, 26, 619-645.

Sue, S. and Smith, R. How Not to Get a Fair Trial. *Psychology Today*, May, 1974, 86-90.

Taillefer, F., Short, E., Greenwood, J. and Brady, R. Video Support in Criminal Courts. *Journal of Communication*, 1974, 24, 111-121.

Chapter VIII

SOCIAL SCIENTISTS AND JURY SELECTION

Overview

THE USE OF psychologists and sociologists to assist counsel in the selection of jurors is a highly charged subject. On one side are those individuals primarily drawn from the ranks of the legal establishment, who are opposed to the concept under any circumstances. They view the application of social science data for these purposes as "jury tampering." It is perceived as an unwarranted intrusion into their private domain. Also, it is threatening, in part, because its impact remains unclear. While not illegal, it is viewed as "stacking the deck."

Proponents, however, start with the assumption that the deck is already "stacked." One critic has commented (Kairys, 1972):

> The history of jury selection in this country quite clearly reveals that vast segments of our population have been denied the right to serve on our juries. Juries have become representative of the white, middle aged, suburban/rural middle class. Black, poor, and young people and anyone who sees a need for basic change in the society—the groups that are most often charged with crimes and most often have their lives placed in the hands of jurors—find virtually no peers on our juries. The one institution through which the framers of the Constitution sought to guarantee that the voice of the community would be heard in the courtroom has been undermined. (p. 801)

Also, their concern as social activists has become galvanized around some recent celebrated cases such as the Harrisburg Seven, Wounded Knee, Joan Little, and Gainesville Eight trials. They sense an "underdog role" for the defense in the face of hostile and at times prejudiced communities. They are also aware of the

167

massive resources available to the U. S. Government in the prosecution of these cases. At times they have been quite successful in documenting bias in jury pools and their survey data have occasionally been employed successfully in change of venue motions. Even critics have grudgingly acknowledged their effectiveness in uncovering biased jury pools. Proponents also point out that what they are doing is perfectly legal; the other side is not prevented from employing similar resources and tactics. Somewhere in between these polarized groups, although close to the proponents, are social scientists interested in the approach itself.

Characteristic of scientists generally, they are curious about the phenomenon. They ask the question, "Does it work and if so, why?" However, these "students" of jury selection, with no apparent vested interest in the outcome, are few in number at the present time.

The early record of success in trials where social scientists were consulted was impressive, as Berk (1976) noted: seven out of nine cases won by the defense. The record since 1975 appears to have been equally impressive. Yet, the overall scientific validity of the approach has yet to be established. This is in large measure due to the many factors that are involved in a trial, but also to the variety of techniques employed by these scientists. Furthermore, some of the trials such as the Harrisburg Seven, Wounded Knee and Gainesville Eight were "political" in nature, and the government is notorious for its inability to obtain convictions in these types of cases.

The variables involved in trials are so numerous that rigorous and systematic evaluation of the approach is virtually impossible. Also, while the use of social science survey techniques is well established and far from being "mystical" as Christie (1976) notes, the "reading" of nonverbal behavior and the general psychological assessment of jurors in the courtroom is apt to vary tremendously, depending on the observer. For most social scientists and attorneys, predicting jurors' attitudes from in-court verbal and nonverbal behavior would appear to be very risky business. A good clinician may not be able to readily translate his training and experience from the clinic to the courtroom.

A great deal of controversy surrounds this issue. Saks and

Hastie (1978) take a dim view of clinical judgments generally and they suggest that the unreliability of clinical judgments extends itself to psychologists' in-court assessments of prospective jurors. They point out that research studies comparing "statistical predictions" with "clinical predictions" have found the latter approach to be lacking in accuracy and reliability. Christie (1979) takes a somewhat different approach. While acknowledging the general weaknesses of the clinical approach, he believes that a well-trained psychologist who possesses a working knowledge of the "person-perception" and authoritarianism literature can learn to apply this knowledge in the selection of jurors.

In general, however, most psychologists, sociologists, and other social scientists lack this necessary background in terms of both theory and practice. Therefore, given the limited expertise presently available, opponents of the use of this approach may be unduly alarmed by the prospect of a social scientist assisting counsel in the selection of jurors. Of course, if this approach survives in the future, both the knowledge and its application may make it a far more potent weapon.

While some practicing attorneys and judges regard the use of psychologists, sociologists and others in jury selection as jury tampering, significant numbers of them, as previously mentioned, recognize that many juries are far from being "impartial" as called for by the Sixth Amendment to the U. S. Constitution (Van Dyke, 1977). As the legal scholar Van Dyke (1977) notes, "Extensive questioning of prospective jurors is aimed at eliminating bias in a jury panel, and it would not be necessary if panels could be presumed impartial in the first place. But in many cases they are not. In cases that generate a high level of emotion, as did the Watergate cases, many prospective jurors have formed opinions about the guilt or innocence of the defendant beforehand, and some effort must be made to ascertain such possible prejudice" (px).

As of this writing there appear to be just a handful of social scientists who, with any regularity, have assisted counsel in the selection of juries. Whether or not this number will increase is problematical, as the phenomenon of "social science and jury selection" has yet to be sculpted permanently into the landscape.

It is too early to tell if it will be accepted on a regular basis into the courtroom. Until now, defense counsel have been the major procurers of the services of social scientists. One of the primary tools, survey analysis, is time consuming and costly. While the celebrated trials such as Wounded Knee often become tainted from extensive pretrial publicity, they also have the advantage of drumming up support, both human and financial, for the defense team. Thus, the jury pool may have to be screened very carefully for prejudice, but the controversial nature of such a trial also serves the interests of defendants.

As Etzioni (1974) noted in an article in *Trial* magazine, "Clearly the average defendant cannot avail himself of such aid. Therefore, the net effect of the new technique, as is so often the case with new technology, will be to give a leg up to the wealthy or those who command a dedicated following. This is hardly what the founders of the American judicial system had in mind" (p. 28). The whole approach has arisen as a result of the inability of the system to function fairly in the first place, and perhaps Etzioni's (1974) reforms are understandable, if not acceptable, in this context. They are as follows: First, if fewer persons were allowed to excuse themselves (and fewer asked to be on it) the universe would be more representative of the community and to a degree less easy to manipulate. Second, that the number of permissible challenges be reduced. Third, he stated that "more powerful, but more problematical action is to extend the ban on jury tampering to all out-of-court investigations of jurors. As examples of this last point, he mentions the collection of data on prospective jurors, interviewing of neighbors, and handwriting analysis. Finally, he points out that, while very controversial, perhaps the judge alone should be allowed to question and remove prospective jurors. This last point may be the most controversial, with most practicing lawyers jealously guarding their rights in this area. Regarding the future prospects of this approach, there are issues that go beyond cost. Legislatures or the court itself may move to severely limit or control the activities of social scientists and jury selection. For some, there is something basically unfair about one side employing such a resource while the other does not.

Two decades ago, Winick (1961) presented his views on the

"psychology of juries" in a text edited by Toch. He viewed the psychoanalytic theory of defense mechanisms as being relevant. For example, he noted that "projection" played a significant role in the behavior of jurors. Projection occurred when a juror attributed some of his own feelings to that of a witness or litigant. This is generally understood to be an unconscious process in which the emotions of the perceiver interfere with his objective evaluation. For instance, if the juror is dishonest in some respect, he may view a particular witness as lacking in credibility. Similarly, "displacement" was described as a mechanism resorted to by jurors. Displacement occurs when feelings experienced toward one person become directed to another. A classic example of this behavior occurs when the husband, who feels angry at his boss but cannot express it directly, comes home and swears at his wife. Everyone, of course, according to this theory, employs these defense mechanisms. The real issue becomes the extent to which this defense mechanism is relied upon. A number of the studies on perception which were reviewed in the eyewitness section of this book apply to an analysis of juror behavior. Generally, with the exception of the last six or seven years, social scientists, and particularly psychologists, have not been active in the area of jury selection.

One of the most interesting studies in this area is one undertaken by Virginia Boehm (1968). She found a relationship between liberalism-conservatism attitudes and jury behavior. She arrived at this understanding as a result of her application of an instrument she devised, the Legal Attitudes Questionnaire (LAQ) to a mock jury sample. The L.A.Q. presented items, in a paper and pencil type of test format, designed to tap authoritarianism, anti-authoritarianism, and egalitarianism. She validated her scale by testing it out on groups such as civil rights workers, who would be expected to be very liberal on a dimension of liberalism-conservatism.

The revised Legal Attitudes Questionnaire was then administered to a large sample of students at the University of California at Berkeley. Two forms of a case, "guilty" and "not guilty," were presented to subjects, and they were required to reach a verdict. The slanting of the case was significantly related to the verdicts reached. The overall results of the study demonstrated a statistically significant relationship between scores on the L.A.Q. and the type of decision reached: authoritarians reached guilty verdicts more frequently. As the author pointed out (Boehm, 1968), limitations existed; the sample may not have been representative of juries generally, and since no group interaction was required, as in real jury deliberations, their decisions may have been affected.

Simon (1967) in her major study reported in her book, entitled *The Jury and the Defense of Insanity,* found that education and ethnicity were two factors that were related to verdicts. Subjects were drawn from jury pools in Chicago, St. Louis and Minneapolis. Jurors listened to recorded trials based on actual cases. Some jurors were presented with a "housebreaking" case while others were exposed to an "incest" case. Specifically, Simon (1967) offered the following statement regarding background characteristics and verdicts reached: "Negro jurors are more willing to vote for acquittal on grounds of insanity than jurors of majority ethnic background; and jurors of higher social status, as measured by educational attainment, are more likely to vote for a guilty verdict" (p. 118) .

The basic rationale for consulting social scientists in the selection of juries is clearly described by Saks and Hastie (1978):

> The theory underlying the core hypothesis, that the characteristics of jurors affect the decision they reach, can be stated fairly simply. A person's demographic background (socioeconomic class, race, religion, sex, age, education, and so forth) denotes a particular kind of socializing history for that person. If you are poor, young, black, and female, you will have been conditioned to view the world differently, to react to it differently, and to hold different attitudes compared with a person who is wealthy, old, white and male. These perceptions, attitudes, and values, in turn, help determine the decision you make as a juror. In addition to demographic characteristics, personality type (whether personality arises through genetics, psychodynamic development, or conditioning history) is thought to predispose a juror to a particular decision. If you are highly dependent on order, for example, you might be conviction-prone. It is unclear whether the theory holds that personality type determines the substantive preference one has, e.g. always wanting to be punitive, or whether it influences the way one processes the evidence (giving more

weight to the government's evidence than to the defense's). Thus, juror demographic characteristics, personality, and attitude are thought to have substantial impact on their decision. (p. 49)

The authors (Saks and Hastie, 1978) go on to point out that the jury selected (jury composition) is affected at two different stages. At the first stage, attention is directed at the eligible pool of jurors (venire) while at the second stage, attorneys are further able to select out jurors during the in-court examinations conducted (voir dire).

Practitioners in the art of jury selection are concerned about the "group dynamics" involved in the selection of any particular group. Who might be expected to be the foreman, etc.? One interesting study which bears on this topic is one conducted by Strodtbeck and Hook (1961). They found that there were three main factors that affected "social distance" among a group of twelve jurors sitting around a jury table: *table length, visual accessibility* and *table width*. They postulated that "social distance" was inversely related to the square root of preferences received. For instance, the selection of a jury foreman comes into play in this regard—the end seating position was selected nearly three times more than it would have been under a statistically even distribution arrangement. Also, end and middle positions contributed a greater amount of "communication" than would otherwise be expected under equal distribution. As common sense would suggest, *visual accessibility* contributed to the behavior of the various parties.

In summarizing the work of Strodtbeck and Hook, Saks and Hastie (1978) found that greater visibility is related to greater knowing of the person, and this increased knowledge has an impact on participation, which in turn appears to affect influentialness.

Procedures in Jury Selection

A review of the techniques available in the arsenal of social scientists engaged in jury selection is offered in *The Jury System: New Methods For Reducing Prejudice* (Kairys et al., 1975). They include the following: *demographic rating system; juror investigation; in-court assessments by experts and defense team members;*

group dynamics analysis.

DEMOGRAPHIC RATING SYSTEM. The authors of the above-mentioned jury manual describe this technique by stating, "Certain personal characteristics or 'demographics' of people make it more likely that they have certain attitudes. This is not the result of chance or accident; characteristics of people, such as race, sex, age, occupation, etc. to a large extent indicate how and by whom they have been socialized and the material conditions that have formed the basis for their perspectives and attitudes" (p. 33).

They go on to point out that it is possible to correlate statistically the relationship between attitudes and characteristics and offer predictions as to how individuals will behave as jurors. Because the relationship between demographic characteristics and attitudes varies from community to community, surveys are required in each trial location if the lawyers are interested in selecting out prejudiced or undesirable jurors.

JUROR INVESTIGATIONS. These are conducted quite often, particularly by prosecutors, and are legal for purposes of jury selection if they do not involve contacting or speaking to potential jurors or their families. The National Jury Project's (Kairy et al., 1975) focus is on the use of a "community network model" as opposed to commercial juror investigative services. The latter approach is described as expensive and not useful unless the investigations are very thorough and detailed in their analysis. The community network approach involves attempting to put together a broad-based group of people who are involved in churches, civic clubs, workplaces, etc. They contact other people who may have knowledge about the potential juror. The use of volunteers to assist in this approach is described by the authors (Kairys et al., 1975) as the most controversial aspect of jury selection. It appears self-evident as to why this may be true.

ASSESSMENTS OF ATTORNEYS, EXPERTS AND DEFENSE TEAM MEMBERS. This technique is many faceted. Observation of nonverbal behavior along with verbal statements are drawn on for purposes of developing profiles of various jurors. Also, minority group members who are assisting the defense team may be particularly sensitive to certain behaviorial nuances that may otherwise escape the notice of professionals when racism may be an issue. Rating scales are sometimes employed. Observers may rate on a one-to-five scale a particular characteristic such as "flexibility" or "conservatism."

GROUP DYNAMICS ANALYSIS. Under this category, the jury manual (Kairys et al., 1975) suggests three features: *leadership, formation of subgroups,* and *bonding or bridging between subgroups.* Much like the individual assessments of jurors, team members pool their observations and analyses for purposes of generating predictions as to how the different individuals will interact as a group.

As already noted, the reliability of these in-court analyses or "clinical judgments" is somewhat suspect and it is not a proven technique that one can place a lot of trust in for purposes of making highly accurate predictions. As previously mentioned, too, there may presently be a few practitioners who combine the requisite theoretical knowledge with courtroom experience who can perform effectively. Because group process analysis is based on inferences drawn from individual verbal and behavioral assessments, it is a weaker model for the prediction of behavior than the individual analysis. In other words, if the individual assessments are flawed, the group dynamics analysis merely compounds the problem.

The key issue involves the level of expertise of the individuals engaged in the assessments. What is their previous record of success? While this is difficult to judge, just as the entire approach is difficult to evaluate, it serves as one criterion for deciding on what experts to employ.

The flavor of the in-court jury selection process is captured by June Tapp's comments of what it was like for herself, as a psychologist, to assist in the Wounded Knee case (Bermant, 1975) :

> I was trying to work with Christie on scoring prospective jurors in terms of their apparent attitudes toward authority. Christie and I scored for authoritarianism, and I assessed the level of legal reasoning of the prospective jurors. Of course, we had rating from my students to increase reliability on these two measures. In particular, we keyed on the responses people made to the judge. Did they seem overly deferential, for instance? How did they respond to questions the judge asked them about the law or the nature of officialdom? While we analyzed the content of their replies we also attempted to assess various kinds of nonverbal cues (p. 63).

Without introducing social scientists into the process, what kinds of questions are generally asked by attorneys during a voir dire? Some very unsystematic observations by the author, in Manhattan Supreme Court, during the voir dire indicated that the following types of questions were asked:

1. Are there any of you who have relatives associated with law enforcement or criminal justice?
2. Is there any reason you believe you cannot be fair in this case?
3. Have any of you been the victim of a crime? If the answer is *yes,* the attorney pursues the matter by inquiring about the feelings the prospective juror has toward the criminal and the event.
4. Tell us a little about yourself, what do you do for a living, are you married, etc.?
5. Will you have any difficulty saying or finding the defendant guilty if you believe beyond a reasonable doubt that he is in fact guilty?

The last question is of particular interest to the prosecution. The fourth question, however, may be the most revealing and useful generally, according to psychologists, due to its open-ended nature. Unstructured questions encourage jurors to express views and feelings that may allow a perceptive observer to infer from the behavior and general character of the prospective juror. Short answers or "yes" and "no" responses do not offer either the defense or prosecution much of a sample of the person's behavior and are therefore much less useful in obtaining a "picture" of the person.

Jury selection techniques have been applied in some of the most highly publicized trials in America. One of these trials involved a Black Panther. Rokeach and Vidmar (1973) discussed this case of jury selection. Factors that affected the make-up of the basic pool of jurors (venire) included: (1) It was based on a 1969 registered voter list; (2) Certain classes of voters were exempted, such as persons over seventy and certain professionals, such as dentists, ministers, lawyers and doctors; (3) Eighteen, nineteen, and twenty-year-olds who became eligible to vote and to

serve on juries following the passage of the Twenty-sixth Amendment on June 26, 1971 were excluded. Defense counsel, the
authors note, chose to call expert witnesses to challenge the assumption that a reasonably unbiased jury could be selected from
juror lists as they were presently constituted in Lucas County,
Ohio. Psychologists in this case focused on the issue of the race of
the defendant, since he was black, and they attempted to point out
through research studies that the racial attitudes of jurors could
affect their verdict. Specifically, the issue was developed by the
presentation of data showing a relationship between characteristics such as age, occupational status, economic status, religious
affiliation, and marital status with racial attitudes. Other areas
identified by the psychologists as "potential sources of juror bias"
included the poverty of the defendant, his status as a "Black
Panther," and jurors' attitudes toward capital punishment. The
authors concluded this short case study by citing a newspaper reporter's articles that suggest that a number of potential jurors were
screened out because of their prejudicial attitudes and thus this
indirectly provided support for the notion that their expert testimony was useful.

One of the most extensive case analyses that has appeared in
published form is the discussion of the Harrisburg Seven case
(Schulman, Shaver, Colman, Emrich and Christie, 1973). The
trial of Father Philip Berrigan and his colleagues in Harrisburg,
Pennsylvania, represented perhaps the first major effort on the
part of a team of social scientists and attorneys to influence the
selection of jurors. The authors repeatedly point out that the
whole approach was untested and was frequently characterized by
a "seat of the pants" approach in which improvisation was the
order of the day. Initially, to the defense team, the deck was
clearly stacked in the government's favor. While a number of
geographical locations were considered, Harrisburg was chosen
for the site of the trial by the government, undoubtedly because
of its conservative character.

A phone survey and then later on an in-depth survey involving
face to face interviews with a subset of the sample revealed a number of important characteristics that researchers felt were critical
in terms of the attitudes these individuals held. For example, re-

ligious affiliation was found to be related to attitudes these individuals would bring to the Harrisburg trial. A critical factor,
in the eyes of the consultants, was the fact that the judge allowed
a great deal of questioning by the attorneys. As a federal judge,
he could have severely limited the questioning. During the three
weeks of jury selection, the defense team, including the defendants, retired to a conference room at the end of the day to compare
their ratings of jurors (1 to 5 scale). One of the attorneys,
through "third-party" contacts, was able to interject additional
information on the prospective jurors. Much of the additional
commentary and description in this article focused on the analysis
of individual jurors that were drawn and the composite profiles
that emerged. Finally, a set of tentative guidelines developed to
assist in similar future endeavors were described. Most of the
points raised have already been discussed in this chapter.

Christie (1976) has replied to critics of jury selection techniques by stating that they "obviously do not know what we're
doing." He goes on to note that there are real limitations in applying social science in the selection of jurors: "There must be
enough ambiguity in the evidence of the case to give a reasonable
juror cause for thought; and the initial composition of the jury
pool must be heterogeneous enough to permit discrimination
among potential jurors" (p. 276). He offered (Christie, 1976) an
example of the problem of lack of *heterogeneity* in the case of
Wisconsin v. Mendoza. In this instance, a seventeen-year-old
Chicano male was accused of murdering two policemen in South
Milwaukee. Without consulting either prosecution or defense,
the judge moved the trial out of Milwaukee to Monroe County
due to "too much pretrial publicity." The problem, however,
posed by selecting a fair jury in this highly rural county was that
the preliminary survey conducted by the defense team revealed
that the county was made up of older, poorly educated whites with
very few professional people among their ranks. Christie (1976)
reported that the jurors empaneled looked uniformly bad (from a
defense standpoint) and that of the twenty-four veniremen who
had been empaneled, only two would have made fair and impartial jurors. Those two were the first individuals "struck" by
the prosecution. In conclusion, Christie (1976) stated, "In my

estimation, under the conditions that prevailed, there was no possibility of obtaining a fair and impartial jury in this case; therefore, any amount of work on jury selection would not have helped" (p. 279).

Another facet of the whole approach, ignored by other writers, has to do with the interactions between social scientists and lawyers (Christie, 1976). Psychologist Christie has observed that criminal lawyers, as opposed to civil lawyers, have a greater interest in juries, and in addition they tend to be on the liberal end of the spectrum. Consequently, they are easier to work with, he suggests. His own experience also leads him to view younger attorneys, who may have backgrounds in sociology and psychology, as more compatible with a social science approach. Finally, he notes that good defense lawyers develop strong egos and aggressive personalities and that their styles of in-courtroom behavior are not unrelated to their behavior with colleagues and other members of the defense team.

In conclusion, jury selection techniques as offered by social scientists appear to have some real value in cases where the evidence is *ambiguous* and where the potential pool of jurors is sufficiently *heterogenous* to allow for discrimination in the selection of individuals. Also, as Saks and Hastie (1978) have observed, the amount and strength of evidence in various cases appear to be far more critical to jury verdicts than the personalities of the individuals selected to sit on juries. Whether or not a particular judge allows defense or prosecution teams leeway in their interviewing of prospective jurors is also critical, as is the general posture of the judge in a given case.

With all of the controversy surrounding the use of social science in jury selection, it remains to be seen if this approach will mature and become increasingly sophisticated over the years, or perhaps will we instead witness a decline of these activities as the result of governmental legislation or intervention by the courts?

REFERENCES

Berk, R. Social Science and Jury Selection: A Case Study of a Civil Suit. In G. Bermant, C. Nemeth, and N. Vidmar (Eds.) *Psychology and the Law*, Lexington, MA: Lexington Books, 1976.

Bermant, G. Juries and Justice: The Notion of Conspiracy Is Not Tasty To Americans. *Psychology Today,* May, 1975, 60-67.

Boehm, V. Mr. Prejudice, Miss Sympathy, and The Authoritarian Personality: An Application of Psychological Measuring Techniques to the Problem of Jury Bias. *Wisconsin Law Review,* 1968, 734, 734-750.

Christie, R. Probability v. Precedence: The Social Psychology of Jury Selection. In G. Bermant, C. Nemeth, and N. Vidmar (Eds.) *Psychology and the Law,* Lexington, MA: Lexington Books, 1976.

Christie, R. "Psychologists and Jury Selection." Lecture offered to Connecticut State Public Defenders as part of a workshop entitled *Legal Psychology,* University of New Haven, West Haven, CT: May 27, 1979.

Etzioni, A. Creating An Imbalance. *Trial,* 1974, 10, 28-30.

Kairys, D. Juror Selection: The Law, A Mathematical Method of Analysis, and A Case Study. *American Criminal Law Review,* 1972, 10, 771-806.

Kairys, D., Schulman, J. and Harring, S. *The Jury System: New Methods For Reducing Prejudice.* Cambridge, MA: The National Jury Project and the National Guild, 1975.

Rokeach, M. and Vidmar, N. Testimony Concerning Possible Jury Bias In a Black Panther Murder Trial. *Journal of Applied Social Psychology,* 1973, 3, 19-29.

Saks, M. and Hastie, R. *Social Psychology in Court.* New York: Van Nostrand Reinhold Company, 1978.

Schulman, J., Shaver, P., Colman, R., Emrich, B., and Christie, R. Recipe For A Jury. *Psychology Today,* May, 1973, 37-84.

Simon, R. *The Jury and the Defense of Insanity.* Boston, MA: Little Brown & Company, 1967.

Strodtbeck, F. and Hook, L. The Social Dimensions of a Twelve-Man Jury Table. *Sociometry,* 1961, 24, 397-415.

Van Dyke, J. Jury Selection Procedures: *Our Uncertain Commitment to Representative Panels.* Cambridge, MA: Ballinger Publishing Company, 1977.

Winick, C. The Psychology of Juries. In H. Toch (Ed.)) *Legal and Criminal Psychology.* New York: Holt, Rinehart and Winston, 1961.

INDEX

181